編集 アルベルト G・ヘッス
村山茂代

版画にみる
明治初期庶民の掟

シアンシア書房

ALBERT G. HESS
and
SHIGEYO MURAYAMA

Everyday law in Japanese folk art

Daily life in Meiji Japan,
as seen through petty law violations:
woodcuts, c. 1878

1980

SCIENTIA VERLAG AALEN

ISBN 3.511.09080.6.

Printed by fotokop wilhelm weihert KG,
Kleyerstraße 12, Darmstadt

Printed in Germany

To

克方

CONTENTS

I. INTRODUCTION

Do some sixty criminal acts of a trifling nature warrant a wide-range introduction that deals with various historical, social, art and legal aspects?

In our day and age, travel to Japan has become accessible to the point of being almost commonplace. The practice of Japanese self-defence sports judo and karate is popular worldwide. Japanese cars, cameras, and appliances are bought and sold in almost all the cities of the World.

In spite of this *rapprochement* between East and West, most of us have really little knowledge of the Far East in general. Are there not some among us who cannot distinguish things Japanese from things Chinese? As Far Eastern history is not being taught in the average Western schools, our knowledge in this area is vague, if it exists at all.

On a more specialized topic, that of crime and criminal law in Japan, there is not much literature in the Western languages. If we know little about the history of crime in our own country, we know still less about the history of crime and criminal law in Japan. Besides these general obstacles to our understanding, petty offenses (contraventions, *Übertretungen*), which we investigate in this book, have hardly ever been focused upon in criminological studies.

There are two reasons why this subject of petty offenses may interest the modern reader. Recent statistics have drawn much favorable attention to Japan in regard to its crime situation. We shall have more to say on this matter below.

Secondly, these petty offenses form a good mirror of everyday life in early Meiji Japan. A modern Western reader can almost "rub shoulders" with the Japanese "little man in the street", watching him commit his minor sins. He is seen in various every day situations: at work, as a pedestrian, rickshaman, traveler, in shrines and temples, in the theater, in the fields and so forth. The traffic problems of today's Kyoto, a city of a million and a half inhabitants, were foreshadowed in the early days of Emperor Meiji. Thus we are dealing not merely with the specific infractions, but their social ramifications as well.

Specifically, this book presents an ordinance for the Kyoto area which was published as a woodcut broadside on December 10 of the "Eleventh year of the Meiji Era", which corresponds to year 1878 on the Western Calendar. The ordinance went into force in 1879. The size of the broadside is about 14 inches by 20 inches (35 cm x 50 cm; see second plate). It consists of a series of seventy separate pictures. The presentation in book form, which renders the individual illustration greatly enlarged, has each of the regulations depicted in graphic detail. The title of the woodcut reads *Kaii Zaimoku Nanajū Kajō* (Minor Law Violations: Seventy Regulations). The artist remains unknown, the publisher was Kampei Ōtani in Kyoto; the price at which the woodcut was sold, 5 sen. The sen was one hundredth of the yen; both denominations represented the newly established currency introduced under Emperor Meiji. Due to inflation the sen has since disappeared (though it is being evoked in many crossword puzzles). At the time five sen was a considerable amount of money.

In the field of art history, to be sure, there is a vast literature on the Japanese woodcut. But our particular pictures were created as an applied art product at the very end of this brilliant history. And it appears that the literature devoted to the particular subject matter, period, and genre of the woodcuts as represented in our book is limited. Even viewing them as an unpretentious product of folk art or of the applied arts of designing, printing and calligraphy for popular consumption, the woodcuts merit some comment from the view point of the art historian.

In view of the considerations noted above, the editors decided in favor of a relatively comprehensive treatment which would attempt to provide the reader with sufficient historical background to assist his understanding of the legal provisions and the social scene in which they were prescribed. Rather than choosing one specialized viewpoint, such as that of the criminologist, the social historian, or the art historian, we tried to strike a balance.

With regard to the social background and milieu, it was helpful that one of the editors grew up in rural Japan and then lived for many years in that country's big cities. She was familiar from her own experience with many of the circumstances referred to in these regulations.

In dealing with legal-historical, socio-historical, and even art-historical considerations, the editors were mindful of the limitations of their own knowledge, as witnessed by the extended list of acknowledgments. Further, in order to avoid pitfalls, a draft of this book was submitted to specialists in various relevant disciplines who have given us the benefit of many greatly appreciated suggestions, as well as their critical, and frank appraisal. Should errors be found in spite of the precautions taken, the editors assume full responsibility for them.

II. HISTORICAL BACKGROUND

Japanese emperors ruled in splendor in the Eighth century A. D. in Nara, the capital; in 794 the court moved to Heian, now Kyoto, where it remained until 1868 (Sheldon, 1973, 214). In the course of the centuries the Emperor lost considerable power to local reigning families who frequently carried on internecine feuds. In 1603, the Tokugawa family established itself as the powerful centralized regime with Tokugawa Ieyasu as *shogun*. While the Emperor played a shadow role at his court in Kyoto, the shoguns of this family ruled the empire de facto from their castle in Edo, through the *bakufu*, their government. During the Tokugawa period (or "Edo period"), the regime became more and more feudalistic. A rigid class structure emerged with the highest stratum formed by the *bushi* or *samurai*, the warriors. At the top were the *daimyos* who were lords of certain regions and had in their service the lower *samurai*. Among the privileges enjoyed by the warrior class was that of arming themselves with two swords. This special attribute can frequently be identified in Japanese paintings and prints. It is not in evidence in any of our woodcuts because the latter were published shortly after the abolition of this samurai privilege. Below the nobility ranked the peasants, next were the artisans, and at the very bottom were the merchants (Sheldon, 1973, 214).

The Tokugawa period lasted until about eleven years before our woodcut was published. This period represented two and one half centuries of peace, with occasional interruptions caused by in-fighting among *daimyos* and by recurrent peasant revolts protesting abuses by their lords. During this essentially peaceful period Japan developed considerably, commercially as well as culturally.

The class that gained most during the Tokugawa period was the lowest, i. e., the merchants. They obtained wealth, and with wealth came power. At the same time, the *shogun's* influence declined until he found himself powerless by the end of the Edo period in the Nineteenth century. By this time also, many *daimyos* and *samurais* had become paupers. Due to their strict honor code, *bushido,* however, they were not supposed to show their poverty. While going hungry, for example, these noblemen were expected to poke their teeth with picks in order to give falsely an impression of just having finished a good meal . . . (Sansom, 1963, 29 f.).

Japan and the West

With the weakening of the Shogunate and the Emperor, Japan began to see threatening signs on the wall. The British victory over China in the First Opium War (1842) aroused great concern. It was realized that Japan's military and naval defenses were no match for the Western powers. In 1853, Commodore Perry, the "peaceful" ambassador from the United States of America – described as "speaking words of peace but looking dangerous" (Sir Rutherford Alcock, 1863, as cited by Toriumi, 1973, 307) – landed without permission from the Japanese Government with an impressive military flotilla of "black ships" in the port of Uraga, near Tokyo, a port forbidden to foreign vessels by the *shogun.*

The Japanese became alarmed. In particular, they were worried that Perry's fleet might interrupt the indispensible food supply for Tokyo. As a preventive measure, the Japanese themselves stopped the run of the rice ships for a while (Sansom, 1963, 234). Perry's statement that he would come back in the following year "with a much larger force" (Beasley, 1972, 89) to discuss "the opening" of foreign trade between the United States and Japan, sounded more like a threat than a peaceful proposal between nations. In 1854, the "shotgun marriage" was consummated. Upon Perry's return, Japan signed one treaty in Kanagawa and a later treaty in 1858 (Beasley, 1972, 238). Both contained many clauses unfavorable to Japan. Perry's mission also brought the Western "blessings" of liquor and the revolver.

Similarly unfavorable treaties with other Western nations followed (Toriumi, 1973, 307). The Prussian minister Graf von Eulenburg, who had arrived in Japan with a fleet of three ships and a contingent of Prussian marines in 1860, was not able to sign a commercial treaty until New Year's Day of 1863, the long delay having been caused largely by the anti-foreigner movement, *Sonno Joi*, that prevailed at that time (see below p. 17).

By now many Japanese began to realize that in order to match the Western nations, Japan herself had to become a modern state powerful in her own right. To provide strong centralized leadership, it was proposed, (not without further bloody in-fighting) that the *shogun* should resign so that the Emperor could become once again the real sovereign of the country. Eventually this was realized in 1867/1868, when the young Emperor Meiji assumed central power and moved his capital from Kyoto to Edo, which became "Tokyo", the "Eastern Capital" (Sansom, 1963, 241).

Japan's contacts with the Occident, however, go back much further than the middle of the Nineteenth century. From 1639 to the time of Perry's arrival, Japan had existed in a state of seclusion. In its extreme form, no foreigners whatsoever were permitted to set foot on Japan, and Japanese were not permitted to leave the country. Even a fisherman, for example, who drifted to another shore in a typhoon could not return to his homeland.

However, prior to the period of seclusion, there had been a period of intense intercourse with Portuguese traders and missionaries. The first Portuguese *carracks*, the "Big Ships" as the Japanese called them, landed in Japan in 1543 (Cohen, 1973, 289), and were welcomed warmly by local lords who wished to enjoy the benefits of foreign trade. Soon the Portuguese became popular with the Japanese who frequently depicted these foreigners and their ships in contemporary paintings. Some Japanese are reported to have enjoyed dressing up in Portuguese costumes.

Missionaries under the leadership of St. Francis Xavier began to arrive in 1549 (Cohen, 1973, 273), and the Japanese, apparently partly in the belief that they could not enjoy the benefits of foreign trade without tolerating the activities of the missionaries, gave them free rein. Relatively large numbers of Japanese were converted to Catholicism. By 1615 the number of Catholics was estimated at half a million persons (Cohen, 1973, 291). For a while all was well. The missionaries rendered the Japanese lords welcome services. In particular, they imported to the Japanese a knowledge of Western science and technology. Among other things, they brought Japan oil painting and engraving, potatoes, the manufacture of firearms, and, possibly, Western construction methods.

Under the *shogun* a centralized feudal state was being formed, based on Neo-Confucianist ideas of loyality to family and to the governing lord. In order to protect the rule of the shogun, it was felt that isolation from the outside world was necessary. The close relations of the missionaries to Europe posed a threat to his power. Thus it was political rather than religious reasons that led to the persecution of the Christians (Miyazawa-Schneider, 1974, 41).

Among the contributing factors was the arrival of two ships: a British ship in 1600, a Netherland vessel in 1609. The British pilot, Will Adams, instructed the Japanese in Western shipbuilding methods (Chamberlain, 1905, 15). Both ships' crew were Protestants, interested only in trade, and not in proselytizing. From them the Japanese learned that it was possible to do business with the West without concomitantly accepting its religion (Cohen, 1973, 291).

Anti-western sentiments became more vigorous and more violent. In 1597 a number of Christians had been executed by crucifixion and in 1622 the mass execution called the "Great Martyrdom", took place (Cohen, 1973, 276). The edict of 1637 established the *sakoku*, the seclusion described earlier, and all Portuguese were expelled.

After 1639 the Netherlanders had a monopoly on trade with Japan (Cohen, 1973, 292), but even they had only a minimum of contact with the population. After 1691, they were only allowed on Dejima, an artificial island in the harbor of Nagasaki. Nevertheless, their influence was great, especially considering the imposed contact limitations.

Japanese cultural life during the Tokugawa period was active and there was a good deal of curiosity about the forbidden outside world. A prime source of information could have been Chinese books, as Japanese intellectuals were familiar with the Chinese language and script. The Shogunate, however, banned many of these books out of fear of Christian propaganda. In 1690 even a guidebook on Peking was burnt merely because it mentioned the tomb of a missionary as one of the monuments of the city (Sansom, 1963, 168–169). Books in the Dutch language, however, were considered less threatening and reached Japan in large quantities through the Netherland traders. Characteristically, two new words appeared in the Japanese language: *rangaku*, "Dutch studies", and *ranbīki*, "Dutch craze". The Japanese became interested in Western objects not merely as rarities and curiosities, but for their application to such subjects as surveying, geography and astronomy (Keene, 1969). From 1741 to 1758, a Netherland-Japanese dictionary was compiled by Konyo Aoki. A Dutch language school was opened in 1789 in Edo (Cohen, 1973, 292). Under the impact of *rangaku*, a Western style exhibition of natural science objects was held in 1759 in that city (Sansom, 1963, 191). In 1770 the first electrical apparatus was built in Japan (Sansom, 1963, 190).

By now some of the aspects of the seclusion were mitigated. The ban on Chinese books had been considerably reduced in 1715. Toward the end of the Eighteenth century a number of contacts with foreign nations took place. Dutch became a kind of *lingua franca* with the Western Nations. In 1860 when the first Prussian Minister Graf von Eulenburg arrived in Japan, interpretation took place still by means of the Dutch language (Kreyher, 1863, 89). There was interest in establishing trade with Russia so that the Northern island of Hokkaido could be developed (Sansom, 1963, 201 f.). From 1797 to 1803 the American vessel *Eliza* visited Nagasaki annually (Sansom, 1963, 205).

However, there were reversals. An expulsion of foreigners was ordered in 1825, and almost again in 1862 (Sansom, 1963, 205, 228, 239). Though a certain friendliness toward foreigners was shown in 1842, it probably stemmed from fears aroused by the British-Chinese Opium War.

The westernization of Japanese military science began in 1841 (Sansom, 1863, 231), and in 1850 a large-scale recruiting of young Japanese for careers in science took place. It is not without interest that this recruitment was made without regard to class distinctions (Toriumi, 1973, 303). In 1855 a foreign studies school was established and in 1856, an institute for the study of foreign documents, as well as village schools were opened in Japan (Sansom, 1863, 233 f.).

During the last years of the Shogunate an anti-western movement, *Sonno Joi* ("Respect the Emperor – Away with Anything Foreign"), waxed again. The *samurais* were especially adamant since those local lords who had begun to westernize their armies did so at the expense of traditional class distinctions. *Sonno Joi* was tied to the popular cause of the restoration of the Emperor which helped considerably to spread anti-foreign feelings. In 1862 these hostile feelings culminated in the above mentioned plan of an expulsion of foreigners, a plan which however was never implemented (Beasley, 1972, 184 f.).

III. THE EARLY MEIJI PERIOD

A keen observer arrived on the Japanese scene not long after the Emperor's restoration to power, a German physician, Dr. Erwin Bälz, who followed a call to Tokyo in 1876 to teach medicine to Japanese students. He noted:

> "... a strange thing is that the Japanese of today do not want to know anything anymore about their past, yes, the educated person is ashamed of it. 'Oh, everything is so barbaric ...,' said one of them and another one, when asked about Japanese history, made it clear: 'We have no history, our history begins only now.'"
> "... These 'New Japanese' infinitely prefer to hear something new praised (even if it is as unsuitable for them as it can be) over something truly valuable from within their own old culture."[1]

Although Bälz was a great admirer of the Japanese, he also had an eye for some of the grotesque aspects of the radical change that was taking place:

> "'Tails' and top hats having been decreed as the official attire for New Year's visits, some characters walk in the streets of the capital who are more comic than any imagination can make them. You poor Japanese who are forced into incredibly bad fitting tails and baggy pants! And on your heads stove pipes that are never the right size! The hands are always in fabulously

1 Bälz himself tried to preserve Japanese tradition by studying sword-fighting (a fact that drew attention in the Japanese press), and by persuading the Japanese authorities to introduce *jiu-jitsu* at the university (Bälz, 1931, 28 f.; Kleinke, 1961, 166 f.).

white gloves, hanging down stiffly, as if they were afraid to touch the suit. But not only men, even boys of ten to twelve years of age become the victims of this craze! And this although the same people would look good – even dignified and noble – in their native garments."[2]

The Meiji period and especially its early years during which our woodcut was published, was one of the most spectacular eras in Japanese history. In 1867 Emperor Meiji, then only 15 years old, began his long reign in Kyoto, the capital. His name was actually Mutsuhito during his life time. Only after his death, the name by which he is now known, "Meiji", was conferred on him. He gained control of his country and within a short time saw it change from a state, on which Western nations imposed unequal and humilating conditions, to a world power. He saw his country make the gigantic economic leap from a medieval feudal economy to a modern industrialized nation and militarily, to a power of first rank. (Fortunately, he could not foresee Hiroshima and Japan's defeat in World War II, perhaps caused by the excesses of a development for which he had laid the groundwork).

Dr. Bälz who became the court physician of the Imperial family described Emperor Meiji as

"... for a Japanese tall and imposing (*stattlich*). He has changed little during the thirty years I have known him. When he appears in public he always wears a uniform, but he does not appear often, having a reserved, almost shy character. He leaves the palace only for certain occasions, such as military reviews, openings and public celebrations, for going on a trip, etc. Otherwise he spends his entire time in the palace, where he lives

2 Trans. from Bälz, 1931, 28–29, 43. – This was in 1876. But in 1905 he had totally revised his opinion. When observing a wedding reception, he wrote: "As I look at the gentlemen who were assembled, I became aware of how well their attire fits and how much they feel at ease now in European costume." (p. 389).

> in a small suite of rooms with a moderately large garden. This garden is separated from the rest of the magnificent imperial park by a high wall."
>
> "Emperor Mutsuhito had the rare luck to always have well qualified and efficient advisers at his side during his long reign. His undoubtedly greatest merit is, however, that he showed himself worthy of these men by trusting them even in spite of the sharpest attacks against them, if once he had recognized their true value" (Bälz, 1931, 434).

Being a young person, he favored change and reform, but, although he warned and acted with reserve at all times against the too rapid adoption of things foreign, westernization progressed, at least until the early 1880's in an almost unbridled fashion.

In 1870 the Tomioka silk reeling factory was opened, the first Japanese enterprise to utilize mass production techniques (Toriumi, 1973, 299). Working conditions were undoubtedly similar to contemporary ones in Europe. Young girls from overcrowded areas worked there for one or two years under what has been described as near-slavery conditions (Koyama, 1961, 13). The establishment of this factory was the beginning of a national textile industry which became Japan's most important, during this early period of industrialization. Not until the early Twentieth century did heavy industry begin and eventually take the lead.

During the first phase of the Meiji era, before 1880, the government frequently took the initiative in founding many state-owned enterprises, from larger ones, to for example such smaller ones as photo studios (Bälz, 1931, 80). Then beginning in 1885 the government divested itself of them and let industries turn to private capitalism (Ishii, 1958, 19).

The year 1872 saw the introduction of compulsory education, military conscription, and Japan's first railroad that started its operations between Tokyo and Yokohama. In

1873 a tax reform took place: henceforth taxes had to be paid in cash instead of in kind (Toriumi, 1973, 303). Japan asserted itself for the first time in 1874 as an imperialist power. Having learned from Admiral Perry, they proceeded to "open" Korea.

We have reached the years immediately preceding the creation of our woodcut. In 1878, the first brewery was opened in Japan (*Kindai Hyaku Nen Shi*, 1967, 22). In the same year Bälz participated in a demonstration of the newly introduced invention, the telephone: "There was always plenty of noise in the contraption, and one could hardly understand anything" (Bälz, 1931, 48).

In 1871 the *daimyo* domains (having briefly become provinces under *daimyo* leadership) were abolished and replaced by a different division, "provinces", whose borders no longer adhered to those of the *daimyo* domains (Toriumi, 1973, 299, 309).

A few years later, in 1877, the *Seinan* (or *Satsuma*) War, actually a rebellion, occurred. As its outcome remained uncertain for some six months and was only quelled by much bloodshed, the entire country was in turmoil. The Satsuma War was the final one of a series of uprisings by unhappy *shizoku*, formerly *samurai*, who had by now lost their class privileges. In the rebellions the *samurai* had partly attempted to fight with swords and other traditional weaponry against the Imperial army which was provided with modern European-style equipment. Kagoshima fell, the fortress of the adherents of the popular general Takamori Saigo and of Shimazu Saburo, former *daimyo* of Satsuma, who were the leaders of the rebellion. Until then, Kagoshima had in effect been a state-within-a-state.

Finally in 1877, the ban on Christianity was lifted and for the first time certain civil rights were granted to the people such as freedom to marry and to choose residence and occupation. In the same year the Western solar calendar replaced the old Japanese calendar (*Kindai Hyaku Nen Shi*, 1967, 23).

In 1878 when our woodcut was created, there was a solar eclipse and a bad rice harvest resulting in high prices.

John Stuart Mill's *The Subjection of Women* dealing with women's rights was translated into Japanese (*Kindai Hyaku Nen Shi*, 1967, 23; Mill, 1869). On December 10, 1878, the ordinance on petty offenses presented in this book was issued. It is interesting that while the month and day of the publication of our woodcut – December 10 – follows the new calendar, the year on the woodcut (eleventh year of the Meiji era) follows traditional Japanese practice.

IV. DEVELOPMENT OF LAW IN JAPAN

Older Japanese penal law is derived from that of China. As far back as one can follow Chinese criminal law, two schools of thought are recognizable. The adherents of Kung-fu-tse, better known in the West under his Latin name of Confucius, believed among other things, that law and ritual belonged together and were an essential part of the social order. Good government was not to be effected through laws that ordered people what to do and what not to do, but by setting good examples and by teaching the people rituals. Taught in this way, it was believed that they could be expected to do the right thing and that they would avoid evil. Proclaiming laws was even considered dangerous as Kung-fu-tse himself had pointed out:

> "If one guides the people by laws, and if one creates order by means of punishment, then the people will evade [the law], and will lose their feeling for decency. However, if one directs the people by means of virtue and keeps order through rites, then the people will preserve their feeling for decency and keep to what is right."[1]

Opposed to the Confucian concept of penal law, the "Legalists" believed in the promulgation of legislation and in the public announcement of laws. The legalists maintained this course of action gave a feeling of security to the population who then knew exactly what was permissible and what was forbidden.

1 We follow, on the whole, for this brief description of the development of Chinese and Japanese law, Tjong (1972), 1088 f. The citation from Kung-fu-tse is translated according to his *Kung-lü* (Conversations), Ch. 4.

The first Chinese codification in the field of criminal law was cast into bronze and made public in 536 B. C. by a legalist, the Minister of State of the feudal State of Chêng. Unfortunately, the text of this code is not known. Even this first penal code was severely criticized by the Confucian follower Shu Hsiang: "The old rulers, when they had to decide about the punishment of a crime, considered the circumstances. They did not produce law books because they were afraid that people would become inclined to conduct law suits for the enjoyment of it (prozeßsüchtig). [Only] when crimes could not be prevented, they set up the bar of justice. [Otherwise] they made efforts to make their subjects reach a moral level equal to their own, the rulers serving as models for the people with respect to practicing the rituals, preserving good faith, and treating the people with humanity ... But when people know that there are law books, they will not respect their superiors. They become keen to dispute (*streitsüchtig*) and to insist on the letter of the law, in the hope that they will win by their argumentation. Then they cannot be governed ... Now, in governing the State of Cheng, you believe that ... you should cast the penal laws in bronze. But will you still be able to keep the people quiet, as I presume you wish? ... I have heard a saying: When a State approaches disaster, its laws multiply" (Translated from Tjong, 1972, 1090–91).

Subsequent centuries – filled with violent internal struggle leading to a breakdown of the Empire into numerous feudal states – apparently demonstrated that the mere teaching by model behavior and instruction in morals and rituals did not suffice to make the Chinese people behave as they should. Historical developments favored the legalistic point of view.

But during the Han dynasty (206 B. C. – 220 A. D.), while law-making in the legalistic tradition continued, the *contents* of the provisions became more oriented toward the teachings of Kung-fu-tse, especially when Emperor Wu (141–87 B. C.) declared Confucianism as the basic principle of government. The climax of this development toward combining the two schools of thought occurred during the T'ang period (618–907 A. D.)

when the great *T'ang-lü* penal code was produced in 624 A. D., and which was then followed by its commentary *T'ang-lü-shu-i* in 653 A. D.

This ecclecticism is evident, for example, in the treatment of the – nowadays basic – legal doctrine of *nulla poena sine lege*. The doctrine states that it is prohibited to punish an act unless a law, stipulated prior to the act, expressly declares such behavior a crime and sets a penalty for its commission. Thus punishment on the basis of analogy is generally forbidden, as is faulty application of the law. Analogy is permissible only when relevant rules do not exist in the code. But the Confucian approach that moral norm is superior to the law is expressed in this somewhat contradictory stipulation: "He who does what he should not do at all, is to be punished by forty strokes with the thin rod" (Art. 62 of the *T'ang-lü* section, trans. from Tjong, 1972, 1094).

The spirit of Confucianism led to the establishment of ten "heinous crimes" for the protection of the cardinal values of this philosophy: the planning of a rebellion, high treason, low treason, the murder of a relative, inhumanity, lack of respect for the emperor and for shrines, lack of piety by children for parents and grandparents, family disputes, disloyalty, and incest (Tjong, 1972, 1095 f.).

Another Confucian feature was the system of the "eight privileges", much criticized by the legalists. Except when one of the heinous crimes had been committed, certain categories of persons and their family members could only be prosecuted by consent of the emperor. If prosecuted, these people usually received a milder punishment. Among those privileged were relatives of the emperor, his confidents, persons of virtue, persons of talent and merit, officials of the higher ranks, dutiful persons, and guests of the government (Tjong, 1972, 1096).

In the T'ang period, four different types of legislative acts were distinguished: codes (*lü*), laws (*ling*), decrees (*ko*), and regulations (*shih*) (Tjong, 1972, 1094; Bünger, 1946, 21). It is the last category which interests us here particularly, because, as Professor Tjong was kind enough to point out to us, the Chinese character for *shih* appears again in our collection of petty offenses promulgated some 1100 years later. Pronounced *shiki* in Japanese, it forms the second part of the term for the more serious petty offenses *i-shiki* of the Meiji period to which we shall refer below.

By this time, Chinese penal law had reached a high level. Professor Dando of Tokyo University considered its state as about a thousand years ahead of European penal law, and quite similar to that of the *Constitutio Criminalis Carolina* of 1532 (Dando, 1959, 357). This monumental codification – addressing the judges, mostly laymen, in the realm of Emperor Charles V – attempted to convey to them the ideas that criminal law was to serve the public interest rather than the interest of the individual complainant, that only a person found guilty under strict rules of evidence should be punished, and that in order to obtain this evidence, torture was permissible only in a strictly limited number of situations and under strict regulation (Schmidt, 1966).

The legislation of the T'ang dynasty was adopted by Japan.[2] This "reception" of Chinese criminal law led – within the framework of the more general *Taika*-Reform (646 A. D.) – to the first Japanese penal code *taihō-ritsu* (702 A. D., not preserved), and to the *yōrō-ritsu* (718 A. D.).

As in the model *T'ang-lü*, there were five types of punishment in Japan, though there is a tendency in the *yōrō-ritsu* toward somewhat milder sanctions. The same system of privileges appears as do the "heinous crimes", but their number is reduced from ten to eight.

However, the *yōrō-ritsu* turned out to be largely unenforceable because Japan at that time and for centuries to come lacked an adequate system of law enforcement. A similar fate was suffered by the *goseibai-shikimoku*, the considerably simplified and very cruel penal code for samurais of 1232. By

2 *See* Clifford, 1976, f. for a more detailed summary of Japanese criminal law.

this time, the power of the emperor had declined in favor of local *daimyos*, who adapted the existing criminal law to local usages.

The long struggle between emperor and *daimyos* ended in 1603 with the victory of Tokugawa Ieyasu (1541–1616) residing in Edo (now Tokyo). Tokugawa was appointed by the emperor as "Barbarian Subduing Generalissimo" (*sei-i-tai-shōgun*), a title better known in its abbreviated Japanese form: *shogun*. As was mentioned earlier in the historical account of Japan's development, the power of the Tokugawa family lasted 265 years, until the Meiji Restoration in 1868 (Beasley, 1972, 430).

Under the Tokugawas a new codification took place, the *kujikata osadamegaki* of 1742. The influence of local usage under the *daimyos* on the legal provisions was especially obvious in its second book, *osadamegaki hyakkajō* or Code of One Hundred Articles. The *kujikata osadamegaki* which remained in force until the Restoration, was not made public but rather considered as directives for judges (Tjong, 1972, 1101; Ishii, 1958, 335).

The early Meiji reformers found the existing criminal law unsatisfactory. They gave priority to penal law reform over the reform of civil law. In the first year, the *kari keiritsu* (1868; Provisional Penal Code) was decreed. In December 1870, another penal code followed, the *shinritsu koryo* (Outline of the New Penal Law), which in turn was replaced by the *kaitei ritsurei* (Amended Criminal Regulations) in June 1873. All three had been considered as only temporary reform measures (Ishii, 1958, 339 f.). The development came to an end when the *Kyu Keiho* (Old Penal Code) was passed in July 1880.[3]

The eagerness of a new regime to present a new criminal code differs considerably from the attitude of many

3 Code pénal promulgé par le Décret no. 36. – The nomenclature is confusing. There is the "New" Code of 1870 – new in relation to the Provisional Code of 1868. Then there is the "Old Code of 1880 which is old, as compared to another "New" Code, that of 1907.

former colonial territories that obtained independence after World War II. It also differs from countries that, since World War II, adopted a socialist form of government. Frequently these countries continue to use for decades the existing colonialist or capitalist codes, with some amendations, to be sure. One reason for the priority given by the Meiji government to penal law reform is that the development of the existing one was considered relatively advanced. Thus the reception of Western law could be effected in this field, without much difficulty (Masunaga, 1948).

Another important reason why Japan placed such urgency on penal law reform was its resentment of the "unequal treaties" which it had been forced to sign with the Western powers since the 1850s. These treaties contained clauses exempting foreigners from the jurisdiction of Japanese courts; foreigners were to be judged instead by special "consular tribunals".

Many of the Western countries had abolished cruel punishment at home a century or less ago. Under the influence of their own reform movements of the Nineteenth century, they became very concerned with judicial safeguards and humane treatment for Europeans in the Far East. They did not want their nationals submitted to the "medieval" practices that still prevailed in Japan and China.

Meiji Japan, on the other hand, was very sensitive to the unequal treatment and tried everything to have the treaties revised. In order to make the foreign powers willing to renounce the consular tribunals, Japan's criminal law and criminal procedure laws needed to be brought in line with Western codifications.

The Outline of the New Criminal Law of 1870 is, on the whole, in the Chinese tradition with hardly anything Western in it (Ishii, 1958, 34). European and particularly French influence begins with the *Amended Criminal Regulations*, as acknowledged in the accompanying edict (Ishii, 1958, 350). In 1873, a French law Professor, Emile Gustav Boissonade de Fontarabie (1852–1910) (Manifestations, 1935, 26 f.) came to Japan at the Japanese government's invitation as a consultant for new codifications. From 1875 to 1880 he drafted a penal code modeled on the *Code Napoléon* (as amended by then). The Napoleonic code was generally considered a model of clarity and precision of expression that had been or was being adapted in a number of European countries, such as Belgium, the Netherlands, Luxembourg and the new German Empire. Boissonade's draft was translated into Japanese, and the *kyu keiho*, the so-called *Old Japanese Penal Code* of 1880, was based on that draft. The *kyu keiho* was in force between 1882 and 1908 when the *keisatsu han shobatsurei*, the New Penal Code of 1907, replaced it (Law 45 of 1907; Tjong, 1972, 1105 f.). The more recent developments lie outside the scope of this study.

The *kyu keiho* of 1880 was actually Japan's first modern criminal code. Among other things, it replaced the traditional Chinese five punishments by the three categories of offenses of the French code, *crime*, *délit*, and *contravention*, – roughly comparable to the Anglo-Saxon concepts of felony, misdemeanor and petty offense (or "violation"). The last – and least serious – of these three groups concerns us here in particular.

Boissonade also drafted a criminal procedure code (1875–1880) and a civil code (1881–1888). His criminal procedure code became a reality in the form of the Old Japanese Procedure Code of 1880, but was quickly replaced by the New Criminal Procedure Code of 1890. His civil code was never adopted.

Eventually Boissonade became quite disappointed about his Japanese legal reform efforts, indeed not one of his great codification projects was in force toward the end of his life (Allix in *Manifestations*, 1935, 4 f.). One limited success, however, is reported. After hearing the outcries of a prisoner undergoing torture in a room adjacent to his own office, his protest to the Japanese government caused torture to be finally abolished in 1879 (Allix in *Manifestations*, 1935, 7 f.; Ishii, 1958, 329).

The reason for Boissonade's lack of success can be found, at least partly, in the political developments of the period. In the early years of the Restoration, Japan and particularly the Japanese jurists had been strongly under French influence. But this influence diminished in the course of time as it was felt that Japan, being an empire, was more akin to the German Empire or the Prussian Kingdom than to the French Republic. France also lost prestige in Japanese eyes after its defeat by the Germans in the Franco-Prussian War of 1870–71. The Japanese Constitution of February 11, 1889 and, eventually, the New Penal Code of 1907 followed the German model.

V. PETTY OFFENSES

Our book, and woodcut, deals with the less serious type of petty offenses referred to as "transgressions of orders", when mentioned in the *shinritsu koryo* of 1870, and the *kaitei ritsurei* of 1873 in sections 287 and 288, dealt with "transgressions of prohibitions, standing orders, or police regulations", punishable respectively by 100, 40, and 20 days of penal servitude. Examples of the first and most serious of the transgressions, against prohibitions, were the breaking or injuring of relics in the great shrines, carrying on a lottery, or illegally[1] torturing a prisoner. Violations of standing orders were the willful evasion of the conscription or lending one's seal to another person. Breaches of police regulations included tattooing of the body, selling adulterated or decayed food or liquor, or obscene books or pictures, passing where "no thoroughfare" was posted, exposing the naked body, cutting telegraph wires, dog fighting, or insolent language used by rickshamen. There were also "improprieties", punishable normally by 30 days of penal servitude – acts which were "clearly in violation of propriety and justice" although there may not be a specific provision applicable (Longford, 1877, 94–95).

In November 1872 *Tokyo ishiki kaii jorei* (ordinance on major and minor violations) for the Tokyo metropolitan area had been issued (Tokyo-shi Shiko, 1963, 690f.). On July 19, 1873, the Council of State made the following decision about the other areas of the country, as announced by its High Chancellor Sanetomi Sanjo (1837–1891):

1 Certain legal forms of torture still existed then. Torture was abolished only in 1879 (Ishii, 1958; see also above p. 29).

"The *ishiki* and *kaii* ordinances for the provinces have been stipulated in accordance with a special bulletin. These ordinances are to be [publicly] announced immediately. However, in case of an adjustment of local conditions or of an increase or reduction [of penalties] – decisions which are left to the discretion of each province –, a petition is to be sent to the police office. That office, furthermore, is competent for giving permission to posting these ordinances [in public]" (reprinted in Kimura, 1877).

Ordinances were then issued on the local level, and among them was that for the Kyoto region with which this book deals.[2] Generally the Tokyo ordinance served as a model for the provincial ordinances but, on the whole, the number of violations in the provinces is considerably increased (Ishii, 1958, 357).

The early Japanese concept of these violations reflected the influence of French law. But it differed from the *contravention* in as much as it distinguished between the more serious *ishiki* (major violation) and the less serious *kaii* (minor violations). In the Tokyo ordinance, the major violations were punishable by ten to twenty blows, while the penalty for the minor offenses was one to two days in jail. Well-to-do persons could pay fines of 75 sen for *ishiki* and 6.25 sen to 12.5 sen for *kaii*. In the provinces, the tendency prevailed to replace flogging by imprisonment and penal servitude (Ishii, 1958, 357).

When the Old Penal Code of 1880 adopted the French triple division of *crimes*, *délits*, and *contraventions*, the distinction between *ishiki* and *kaii* was abolished, and only one term *ikeizai* was used (art. 425–430) (Ito, 1966, 15). It grouped them, though, into five categories according to the penalties, which ranged from 3–10 days of detention, fines between 1 *yen* and 1.95 *yen*, to fines between only 5 *sen* and 50 *sen*. No

2 There is also *Ishiki kai zukai*, with comments by Nobuaki Kimura (1877). For Nagoya, as another example, see Imae, 1878.

equivalent detention was stipulated in case of non-payment of the fine.

Our woodcut deals exclusively with *kaii*, the minor violations, as they were prescribed for the Kyoto region. It does not mention any sanctions, but we know that *kaii* were punishable by fines from 5 to 70 *sen* (Kimura, 1877, art. 2). *Ishiki* are mentioned once, in plate 70, and this reference does not appear to make much sense.

In the 1870s the modern concept of division of powers in the government was not yet implemented in Japan. Petty offenses were dealt with by the police who acted as law-enforcers as well as judicial agents.

VI. CRIMINOLOGICAL OBSERVATIONS

In modern criminal codes, the principle prevails that ignorance of the law does not protect a violator against punishment. In the old Chinese-Japanese tradition this may not have been considered a problem. As has been described above, the Confucianists did not believe in written law. Even when laws were issued, they were sometimes regarded as internal instructions for judges and no publication took place.[1] As late as 1868, the Provisional Law was not publicly announced, and when the New Penal Law of 1870 was issued, the Japanese government hesitated for a number of months before granting permission to print the text for general distribution. But once the Japanese government – generally inclined to propagandize its reforms – had become convinced of the need for publicizing laws, it gave publication particular stress. This was especially true when the laws concerned were petty offenses.

The publication of legal texts was then and is still usually done, as in most countries, in a law gazette which, although available to the general public, is hardly ever read by anyone except lawyers and officials. It is reasoned that by publishing the law in a gazette, every citizen is being given the opportunity to know the law and therefore cannot claim ignorance of it. In general, the publication of a law by means of a law gazette appears ineffective. In particular, it does not serve a universally recognized purpose of criminal law, general deterrence, which can only take place when there is no ignorance about what is permissible and what is forbidden. This applies especially to petty offenses, with its large number of provisions dealing with matters that are not clearly "right" or "wrong" from the viewpoint of society's value system.

1 See above, p. 24.

It is interesting that Japan adopted the cartoon as an effective means of propagating the law. In a sense, Japan's use of cartoons for the dissemination of *kaii* appears very modern. One important reason for this popular medium to be used is that although compulsory education had been decreed in 1872, by 1878 it had not yet been widely implemented. Thus, there were many illiterates among the population to whom the government wished to make known the legal provisions.[2] But in the West the use of cartoons for this purpose is not as old as in Japan, and dates back perhaps only some fifty years. And even today, the use of cartoons as a means of legal instruction occurs mostly in the private sphere, that is in industry and business. Factory security regulations, as an example, are sometimes conveyed to workers by means of cartoons. Department stores also display occasional warnings against shoplifting in the form of cartoons. Little use of cartoons, though, is made by authorities to publicize legal provisions. The New York City Transit Authority put up posters in subway stations in the early 1960s that depicted in small humorous sketches, types of behavior forbidden in subways, such as littering or smoking cigarettes. The United States Government has also used cartoons to impress on young persons the consequences of drug abuse. But such users remain exceptions.

Woodcuts were not the only medium used in Meiji Japan for propagating the knowledge of the *ishiki* and *kaii* regulations. There was also, for example, a ditty sung to the tune of a then popular *kazoe uta*, the "Counting Song". The following is a free translation of a selection of verses:[3]

2 See above p. 21; school budgets had been drastically cut because of the Satsuma War. – Japanese School (1878), 663.

3 Altogether there are thirty-two verses; Yoshino (1929), 11 f.

2. This is Number Two:
   Rickshas two that go along
   Pulling side by side
   That can only mean one thing:
   Trouble with police!

3. This is Number Three:
   More and more of dirty dust
   Makes a mighty mound:
   Petty violations are
   Seed for bigger crime!

4. This is Number Four:
Unlimited, dirty greed
Craves for endless gain,
But you should not dare to hawk
Spoil'd and smelly carp!

5. This is Number Five:
Never anyone should throw
Even out of fun
Into rice fields cared with love
Stones, sticks and so forth!

19. This is Verse Nineteen:
Fire breaks out, but you don't help,
Sleeping with your wife.
What a foolish thing to do
Foolish, bet your life!

20. 'Tis the Twentieth Verse:
If you do not have the cash
Twenty whacks you get,
But with wealth, all that you pay
Only sev'nty five.[4]

. . . . .

As can be seen, the stipulations in verses 2 and 5 correspond to those in plates 6 and 38.

In criminology, petty offenses have received only limited attention, at least not *qua* petty offenses. A few specific ones have been discussed: vagrancy, mendicity, prostitution, and drunkenness. Even the criminological study of traffic offenses, to which attention has been drawn only lately, does not usually deal with the *minor* traffic violations. Studies on traffic offenses tend to center on more serious crimes such as negligent homicide by driving, reckless driving, or driving under the influence of alcohol.

Furthermore, not only the criminology but the history of traffic offenses is still largely unexplored. Therefore the relevant pictures of our woodcut may be of particular interest. Streets in early Meiji Kyoto were sometimes lined with trees, and occasionally had modern European-style street lamps. They also served as depositories for garbage and dead animals, medicine seeds, grains, and, maybe as places where fishes were laid to dry. Traffic was mainly by human force, or by horse and cattle. Large animals were sometimes allowed to run around freely in public places. But one recognizes the beginnings of the traffic problems of modern Kyoto and of the large metropolitan

4 Freely translated by the editors.

city in general: blocking traffic, speeding, the need for protecting the weak vulnerable pedestrian in narrow streets.

No doubt, one reason why little attention has been given to petty offenses is their trifling nature, but this is regrettable. These offenses are by no means criminologically unimportant. Drunken persons and others who cannot afford to pay the fines imposed on them may be inappropriately exposed to all the negative factors connected with imprisonment: stigmatization by society; bad influence from other prisoners; and so forth. To a great extent petty offenders account for the overcrowding of jails in many countries.

Another explanation for the lack of criminological interest in petty offenses may be that they are not listed in many crime statistics, therefore data are not easily available for study. But this is a flimsy reason, since criminological research hardly makes use of official statistics anymore due to the many reservations voiced against them. Studies of specific petty offenses based on representative samples could no doubt be undertaken without undue difficulty in most countries.

As a group, however, petty offenses lack uniformity. They comprise everything from violations of a sanitation code to the obstruction of traffic; from drunkenness in public to unlicensed soliciting. Motivations for and situations under which petty offenses take place vary extremely. Therefore it is almost impossible to come forward with valid generalizations about them.

One aspect which all petty offenses have in common is that the law clearly distinguishes them as less serious than "common" crimes, such as murder or theft. The sociological concepts of "primary" and "secondary" deviance may help to clarify this distinction (Yinger, 1960, 625 f.). The person who shows only primary deviant behavior does break a norm, but his conduct is not considered so intolerable that he is cast out from his group. Both the group and the offender himself continue to see him as a group-member in good standing. By contrast, secondary deviant behavior – which not only comprises the common crimes but also a number of other forms of deviancies – is so intolerable that the offender becomes excluded from the group by such punishments as imprisonment or the death penalty.

Petty violators are generally considered primary deviants. Only rarely is such an offender considered an "outcast", although such stigmatization occurs especially with vagrants and prostitutes. These considerations may also apply to Meiji Japan. It stands to reason that *kaii*, and probably also the *ishiki*, were considered trifling offenses and that punishment for their commission did not lead to a loss of status in the society for the offender.

In fact, it stands to reason that a good deal of the behavior depicted as officially undesirable in our woodcut was not of great concern to the Japanese people at large. Urinating in the street or the transport of excrements in the street probably did not seriously disturb the Meiji Japanese. The rationale behind some of the provisions may well have been the wish to appear "civilized" to the Western countries. The reader is reminded of those unequal treaties with the West, mentioned earlier, and Japan's desire to eradicate everything that could make them appear to outsiders as "barbarians".

For similar reasons they may have introduced prohibitions in other ordinances that deal with *ishiki*, against: tatooing, communal bathing of the sexes, and so forth. They even made it illegal to break off branches from trees in public parks and on streets, which conflicted with a long established tradition. In autumn the Japanese people like to bring home red-leaved maple branches and compose poetry about them.[5] Nevertheless, these considerations need not minimize the fact that the majority of the offenses listed were aimed at protection against *bona fide* nuisances that existed.

5 We are grateful to Mr. Beermann, University of Freiburg i. B., Federal Republic of Germany, for these insights (unpublished letter from him of 8 December 1977), and for many other suggestions.

Another motivation for the ordinance is expressed in the third verse of the above ditty (see above, p. 36), namely the idea that small wrong-doing may pave the way for more serious crime. We are reminded of the "status offenses" in many of the juvenile court laws of the Twentieth century which forbid certain behavior to children that would not be an offense for adults: truancy, smoking tobacco, drinking alcohol or running away from home, and so forth. Here too, the reasoning appears to be that such behavior may lead to a life of crime. Just as the influence of status offenses on the criminal careers of youngsters has not been proven, it may be assumed for Meiji Japan that the commission of the *kaii* in our woodcut would seldom be the prelude to a criminal career.

Perhaps this line of thinking is the result of mistaking what is believed to be the consequences of a pre-delinquent act with the consequences of its consequences. To-day it is believed that a certain amount of pre-delinquent (even delinquent) behavior is normal for an adolescent and does *not* lead to a career of crime. However, a youngster may be caught after committing such an act; he may be officially labeled by a juvenile court as a delinquent, experiences stigmatization and perhaps incarceration in an institution where he may join the inmate subculture. Not so much the delinquent act but all the consequences may contribute then to a career of crime. Petty offenders (e. g. drunkards) who are jailed because they lack the money to pay a fine may undergo similar experiences. These observations, to be sure, apply to today's juveniles and petty offenders. Only future research will show whether they are also valid as regards Meiji Japan.

Attention has recently been drawn to the very favorable crime situation in present-day Japan:

> "... An individual is ten times more likely to be murdered in the United States than in Japan; thirteen times more likely to be raped; and six times more likely to be the victim of theft ... The likelihood of being robbed

in the United States is 208 times greater than in Japan" (Bayley, D., as quoted in Japan Society, 1977, 1).

While the crime situation in Japan appears favorable, such direct comparisons are questionable. Comparisons of crime figures from one country to another – it is generally recognized by criminologists – are impossible, due to the wide differences in criminal law, criminal procedure, police forces, court structure, intensity of prosecution, statistical registration systems, and – last but not least – social mores. Criminologists have been struggling with this problem for about a hundred years without great success.[6]

In addition to these general difficulties of international crime statistics, Japan poses its own brand of difficulty. Professor Tokoro studied the reporting of crime and delinquency to the police in a Japanese fishing village, Esahi, in 1962:

> "It was noted by the police that crimes and delinquencies committed by village residents were not reported and that the villagers were quite reluctant to do so or to give information to the police concerning them. Consequently, the police tended to handle only those crimes committed by day laborers from other communities. Also, the police kept few records of crimes committed by local residents, even though they knew of many such crimes" (Tokoro, 1970, 10).

It was found that crimes and delinquencies committed by members of the Esahi community were being handled directly and informally within that community. Only offenders from outside the village were reported to the police. On the other hand, when Professor Tokoro visited the United States, he was much surprised to find that delinquent youngsters were

6 Hess, 1959; Bollmann, 1973; International Police Organization-INTERPOL, various years; see especially the detailed reservations by INTERPOL about the use of these statistics. Lately the United Nations claims to have achieved better results, but as their methodology is not published, a judgement is not yet possible. (United Nations, 1977).

brought to the attention of the authorities, regardless of their place of residence or background. He was also surprised that reporting took place even for trifling offenses, and in particular for non-criminal "status offenses" such as truancy or running away (Tokoro, 1970).

We cannot go further into the role of the community in matters of crime, but it is obvious that crime statistics are drastically altered when only crimes committed by outsiders are reported. This factor alone may account for much of the higher official crime statistics in the United States than Japan.

More promising than direct comparisons of crime figures from one country to another are comparisons of *trends in crime*. Here indeed Japan's situation appears to be sound, as shown in table I. As the crime rates indicated through the years, there has been a steady decrease from 1948 to 1973, and even the figures for 1974 and 1975 show increases so minimal that one can only speak of a "leveling off". Such a decreasing trend is most unusual for the countries of the Western World where a large number of them have shown considerable increases in approximately the same period. Only a few countries, such as Denmark and Switzerland can boast of favorable trends similar to Japan.

TABLE I

Non Traffic Penal Code Offenders in Japan, Crime Rates Computed per 100,000 Criminally Responsible Inhabitants

Year	*Crime Rates*
1948	2,995
1955	2,337
1966	1,690
1969	1,570
1970	1,587
1971	1,526
1972	1,473
1973	1,416
1974	1,425
1975	1,428

(Adapted from: Japan Ministry of Justice, 1977, Table 1, page 2)

This is not the place to discuss in detail the trends of crime. Explanations have been offered for the low figures in Japan, such as the fact that considerable trust is given to authority in Japan, and especially to the police. There are also differences in police behavior and a closer integration of the police into the local Japanese community. The community shows greater responsibility for the behavior of its members as well as for their welfare (Clifford, 1976, 1977; Japan Society, 1977; McKay, 1977).

One of the editors had an opportunity to witness the important role of the local community when undertaking a report on the Japanese volunteer parole and probation officers (*hogoshi*) in 1970 (Hess, 1969, 1970 a–c). Even in the large cities, community organizations for the various city quarters effectively care for community affairs, in particular, for criminals and former criminals.

Incidentally, the above described favorable trend does not apply to modern traffic offenses, which form a considerable part of our old *kaii*. The Research and Training Institute of the Japanese Ministry of Justice explains this fact by pointing at the disproportionate increase in motor cars and motor cycles in that country (Japan, 1977, 1,43).

Whether we deal with differences in crime trends in general or only traffic offenses, further study is suggested, a study which should include the history of crime and particularly the history of traffic offenses in the period of our woodcut with its beginnings of modern traffic problems.

VII. ART-HISTORICAL CONSIDERATIONS

The Japanese woodcut derived from Chinese art probably in the Seventh century (Hempel, 1963, 9), long before printing started in the Western World. A long line of traditions developed during its twelve hundred year history. One characteristic common in both Far Eastern painting and the woodcut print was extreme simplification, a feature easily recognizable in the pictures of this book. Such simplification can be observed in Chinese painting a thousand years earlier which was to influence Japanese graphic art strongly. This very element of design is kindred to the spirit of Zen Buddhism – so popular in Japan – which emphasizes simplicity and restraint for obtaining *satori*, a mystic, "direct" perception of the world (Munsterberg, 1965, 17). Designs that leave out everything unessential and exaggerate the essential in caricature-like fashion are indeed suitable for the purposes of an "immediate", spontaneous understanding by the spectator. The Zen-inspired landscapes as well as the frequent portraits of priests and sages of the Kamakura period (1185–1392) are good early examples of these characteristics (Munsterberg, 1957, 92 f.).

The Japanese woodcut, while adapted from Chinese art, played only a modest role as an art form in the courtly medieval culture. It became the most important art mass medium in the Edo period, appealing to the, by then, affluent and art-hungry citizenry. Although it derived from painting and always kept close contact with that art form, it developed its own characteristics. For example, early Japanese painting, following the model of Chinese art, was distinguished by "framelessness". Human figures, animals, flowers, trees, entire landscapes and historical scenes appeared on scrolls and screens surrounded by blank space. In contrast, the woodcut demanded "a background of clear lines and spaces". Thus, lines marking the outer limitations of the picture contributed to making its structure clear (Hempel, 1963, 12).

The difference in the approaches to the graphic arts in the West and the East is aptly described in a Chinese anecdote. Castiglione, a Jesuit priest (1688–1766) found his way to Peking under Emperor Ch'ien Lung. He became a Chinese court painter, and was famous for his porcelain decorations. The Emperor directed him not to paint in the European manner but to paint in Chinese style: "The imperfections of the eye . . . [afford] no reason why the objects of nature should . . . be copied as imperfect."[1] The emperor was aware of the fact that Far Eastern art interprets the objects "through the mind", while the Western artist paints them as the human eye sees them. An example would be parallel lines extending from foreground to background. The Japanese traditional artist may use "parallel perspective", drawing the lines parallel assured by the knowledge that receding lines remain parallel in the objective sense, while Western "central perspective" will show them converging in reference to a "vantage point" – the location of the onlooker's eyes. Central perspective renders the three-dimensional world of reality in the two dimensions of the painting or woodcut by correcting the shortcomings of the human eye. The Far Eastern painter ignores these shortcomings.

Western art was not unknown to the Japanese. Since the days of the Portuguese they had been exposed to it. Western central perspective was introduced into the Japanese art of the woodcut in the course of *rangaku* by Okumura Masanobu (1686?–1764), at a time when Japanese painters eagerly studied Western engravings (Hempel, 1963, 14). Hokusai and

1 Quoted (as an event that had happened in the past) by John Barrows (1806; – Barrows, accompanied the British ambassador to Peking in the 1790s and set up the astronomical clock that was given to the Chinese emperor at that occasion. Cited according to Hsiang, (1976), 176. On Castiglione see Hobson (1915) I, 205; Scheurleer (1974), 74, 81.

Hiroshige, among others, made effective use of the technique of central perspective, but the creator of our woodcut, it appears, pays little heed to it. There is a timid beginning toward central perspective, for example, in the lines of the roof in plate 12. But on the whole, our artist adheres to the traditional "parallel" perspective (see for example plates 13, 16, 58). In view of the widespread use of central perspective in Japan in the Eighteenth and Nineteenth centuries, the holding back of our artist to the older form appears archaic, and points at the conservative nature of folk art. Folk art generally tends to cling to established stylistic patterns long after the leading artists of the times have given them up.

It is unnecessary here to deal with the different schools that played important parts in the development of the Japanese woodcut. The most famous of these schools was no doubt the *ukiyo-e* school, which created *genre* painting devoted to the transient beauty of the "fleeting, floating world" (Lane, 1962, 10 f.), a world populated by courtisans, actors and wrestlers. Hedonistic pleasures of this life were depicted, among them the gay quarters, the popular festivals, the enjoyment of music, the bath, the viewing of cherry blossoms and the catching of glow-worms.

One aspect of the *ukiyo-e* tradition, is its preoccupation with the common people. The leading example in this tradition is, perhaps, Hokusai's *Manga*, with its thousands of folk scenes (Kondo-Grilli, 1955; Michener, 1958). Hokusai's pupils and Hiroshige and his followers skillfully continued the tradition of filling the landscapes with a multitude of plain people.

This interest in the ordinary people reflects the rise and growing affluence of the public that bought woodcuts, especially the merchants. Traditionally the lowest class, they had gained wealth and status and acquired cultural tastes. Hindered by the severe travel restrictions imposed by the *shogun* from visiting the places depicted, merchants bought and enjoyed landscape woodcuts (Takahashi, 1972, 12). Thus the artist's concern for the people was only natural. A political parallel to the artist's interest in the common man may be found in the "Respect for Public Opinion" movement which eventually led to inclusion of the idea of a government based on public opinion in the "Five Articles of the Imperial Oath" of 1868 (Toriumi, 1973, 309; Koyama, 1961, 11).

Being a mass medium, the woodcut served – at least from the Seventeenth century on – commercial purposes. It was produced for the market. In spite of commercialization, its high artistic level remains remarkably constant. As a commercial product, it involved the collaboration of several persons. The most important one was the artist who designed the sketches, and indeed many of the great Japanese artists designed woodcuts. An engraver then carved the sketches into wooden blocks. He, or someone else, took care of the printing. And last but not least, a publisher promoted the sale of the print. He also directed the trade organization *jihon don'ya* to which all those who participated in the production belonged (Takahashi, 1972, 13).

A great deal of most exquisite art was created in the woodblock print. At the same time the woodcut remained a true folk art (Munsterberg, 1957, 152). Many of the prints were created by unknown craftsmen who, while pursuing practical rather than artistic goals, had remarkable skills and applied their age-old traditions. And from the days of the *ukiyo-e* (Hempel, 1963, 11), the consumers were, as has been noted, the general populace.

In the Meiji period Japanese and Western art began to mingle. The international exhibitions held in London (1862) and Paris (1867) had great influence on Impressionism. Artists such as Manet, Monet, Degas, Gauguin and Toulouse-Lautrec received new stimulus from Japanese art (Narasaki, 1966, 188). Western style painting was introduced to Japan under the designation of *yōga*. An Englishman, Charles Wirgman, self-taught pictorial correspondent of *The Illustrated London News,* gave instruction in Western painting in Yokohama in 1859. He taught specifically oil and water color painting. There were also private *yōga* studios under the direction of Japanese artists, such as Yuichi Takahashi's Tenkai-ro (Harada, 1974, 15f.; s. a. Munsterberg, 1978).

The Meiji reform which was to radically affect the Japanese way of life was propelled by widespread propaganda. As has been documented, obligatory schooling and general literacy were only beginning and the development of Western-style newspapers was yet in its infancy. Propaganda for reform measures thus made extensive use of the easily available and highly developed medium of the Japanese woodcut (*Ibid.*).

At this time the publishing of woodcut prints flourished as never before. There were 120 publishers, "by far the greatest number in the entire history of woodblock publishing in Japan" (Narasaki, 1966, 186). However, eventually the revolutionary force for change extended to all fields of human activity, including the fine arts. For the Japanese woodcut this meant the beginning of the end. Photography – promoted in government-operated studios (see above, p. 20 and plate 61) – and other modern means of reproduction in time took the place of the old art.

The publisher of our woodcut is known, but the engraver and the designer are not. The latter may indeed have been an humble artisan as those described above, eking out his living in the service of the publishers. But he had talent mastering his lines and being able to limit himself to the essentials. He also had an eye for the human shape and human movements. Furthermore, he was capable of creating complete compositions in a very small space. Each picture of the original woodcut equals only approximately the size of four ordinary postage stamps.

As to the iconography of the representations, normally the forbidden behavior described in the text is depicted (e.g. plates 5, 10, 51). Occasionally, it is the contrary: the artist shows the approved behavior, as in plate 68. Plate 13 shows a person studying the regulations. In certain other cases the contents of a regulation is symbolically represented, frequently in accordance with the principle *pars pro toto*. Thus e. g. in plate 67 which deals with traveling, only a traveler's hat and a passport are shown.

Calligraphy, for the Japanese, is not separated from pictorial art, contrary to Western concepts. The Japanese word *kaku* means "to write", as well as "to draw" and "to paint". Calligraphy is generally considered as respectable an art as painting. Our artist also shows skill as a calligrapher. His task is not easy. He sometimes has to accommodate a relatively long legal text in the limited area at his disposal. Noteworthy is the way he juxtaposes script and pictorial areas in a variety of ways, showing remarkable imagination with respect to their shapes and positions. Thus, in plates 2 and 12 where the moon and the rising sun appear above the dark calligraphy, the script areas are used to suggest the dark sky and in plate 47, to suggest a body of water.

BIBLIOGRAPHY

Alcock, Sir Rutherford 1863 — The Capital of the Tycoon: A Narrative of Three Years Residence in Japan. London. (reprinted 1973. Westport, Conn., Greenwood Press).

Allix — see *Manifestations* 1935.

Ballon Monté — see Thompson, Reuben R. 1975.

Bälz, Erwin 1931 — Das Leben eines deutschen Arztes im erwachenden Japan: Tagebücher, Briefe, Berichte. Stuttgart: J. Engelhorns Nachf.

Barrows, John 1806 — Travels in China (as cited in Hsiang, 1976, 176).

Bayley, D. — see Japan Society 1977.

Beasley, W. G. 1972 — The Meiji Restoration. Stanford, Calif., Stanford University Press.

Boissonade de Fontarabie, Gustave Emile — see *Manifestations* 1935.

Bunger, Karl 1946 — Quellen zur Rechtsgeschichte der T'ang-Zeit. Peiping, Catholic University.

Chamberlain, B. H. 1971 — Japanese Things. Rutland, Vermont and Tokyo, Charles E. Tuttle. (originally published under the title *Things Japanese*, circa 1905).

Clifford, William 1976 — Crime Control in Japan. Lexington, Mass., D. C. Heath & Co.

1977 — "The Japanese Way with Crime", in *Justice of the Peace*, January 8, 1977.

Cohen, Paul A.
1973 "Europe Goes East: The First Impact of the West on China and Japan", in Toynbee (1973), 263–292.

Dando, Shigemitsu
1959 "Die Strafrechts- und Strafprozeßrechtswissenschaft in Japan". In *Goltdammer's Archiv für Strafrecht* (12): 357–367.

Gollmann, H. J.
1973 Internationale Kriminalstatistik: Geschichtliche Entwicklung und gegenwärtiger Stand. Stuttgart, Ferdinand Enke Verlag.

Harada, Minoru
1974 Meiji Western Painting. Adapted by Bonnie F. Abiko. New York & Tokyo, Weatherhill / Shibundo.

Hempel, Rose
1963 Holzschnittkunst Japans: Landschaft-Mimen-Kurtisanen. Stuttgart, Chr. Belser Verlag.

Hess, Albert G.
1959 Criminal Statistics: Standard Classification of Offences – Report by the United Nations Secretariat. New York.

1969 "The Japanese Volunteer Probation Officer System: First Thoughts" (in Japanese), in *Tokyo Hogokansatsu*, May 1969.

1970 a "The Volunteer Probation Officers of Japan", in *International Journal of Offender Therapy*, 14: 8–14.

1970 b "Der Gebrauch von Volontären in der japanischen und amerikanischen Bewährungshilfe" in *Bewährungshilfe*, 17 (3): 192–195.

1970 c "Japanese Volunteer Probation and Parole Officers (in Japanese), in *Hoseihogo to Hanzaiyobo*, 16: 18–25.

Hobson, R. L.
1915 Chinese Pottery and Porcelain: An Account of the Potter's Art in China from Primitive Times to the Present Day. New York & London, Funk & Wagnalls and Cassell & Co. (reprinted New York, Dover Publications, 1976).

Hsiang, Ta.
1976 "European Influences on Chinese Art in the Later Ming and Early Ch'ing Period", in *Renditions*, (16): 152–178.

Imae, G.
1878 — Ishiki Kaii Zukai (A Presentation of light and more serious petty offenses). Nagoya (See Meiji Bunka Zenshu, XIII, 105–117).

International Criminal Police Organization-INTERPOL
various years — International Crime Statistics.

Ishii, Ryosuke
1958 — Japanese Legislation in the Meiji Era. W. J. Chambliss, trans. Tokyo, Kasai Publishing & Printing Co.

Ito, Shigeki
1966 — Kei Hanzai Ho (The Law of Petty Offenses). Tokyo, Tachibana Shobo.

Japan
1880 — Code pénal promulgué par le Décret no. 36. Tokyo, Imprimerie impériale.

Japan. Ministry of Justice. Research and Training Institute
1977 — Summary of the White Paper in Crime 1976. Tokyo.

Japan Society
1977 — The Police and the People: A Comparison of Japanese and American Police Behavior. New York, Japan Society.

A Japanese School
1878 — *Harper's New Monthly Magazine*, (341): 663–666, October.

Keene, Donald
1969 — The Japanese Discovery of Europe, 1720–1830. Revised edition. Stanford, California, Stanford University Press.

Kimura, Nobuaki
1877 — Ishiki kaii zukai (Lighter and more serious petty offenses). Illustrated by Beizei Kubota. Kyoto, Kawakatsu & Umemura.

Kindai Hyaku Nen Shi Nen Pyō (History of the Last Hundred Years). Tokyo,
1967 — Mainichi Shimbunsha.

Kleinke, Arno
1961 — Die geschichtliche Entwicklung des Jiu-Jitsu und Judo, in *Zeitschrift für Strafvollzug*, 10: 162–168.

Kondo, Ichitaro & Elise Grilli — Katsushika Hokusai (1760–1849). Rutland,
1955 — Vermont, Charles E. Tuttle.

Koyama, T. 1961 — The Changing Social Position of Women in Japan. Paris, UNESCO.

Kreyher, J. 1863 — Die preußische Expedition nach Ostasien in den Jahren 1859–1862: Reisebilder aus Japan, China und Siam. Hamburg, Rauhes Haus.

Lane, Richard 1962 — Masters of the Japanese Print: Their World and Their Work. Garden City, New York, Doubleday & Co.

Longford, Joseph H. 1877 — A Summary of the Japanese Penal Codes. Transactions of the Asiatic Society of Japan, 5, pt. 2.

Manifestations commemoratives en l'honneur du Professeur G. E. Boissonade. 1935 — Tokyo.

Masunaga, G. 1948 — Keihanzai-Ho Kaisetsu (Explanation of the Law on Petty Offenses). Tokyo.

Mc Kay, Robert S. 1977 — Japan: Streets without Crime, Disputes without Lawyers, in *Bulletin of the Japan House* (New York), 24 (9): 1–6.

Michener, James A. 1958 — The Hokusai Sketch-Books: Selections from the *Manga*. Rutland, Vermont, Charles E. Tuttle.

Mill, John Stuart 1869 — The Subjection of Women. London.

Miyazawa, Koichi & Hans Joachim Schneider
1979 — "Vergleichende Kriminologie: Japan", in *Handwörterbuch der Kriminologie*, Ergänzungsband, 1–46. Berlin, De Gruyter.

Munsterberg, Hugo
1957 — The Arts of Japan: An Illustrated History. Rutland, Vermont, and Tokyo, Charles E. Tuttle.
1978 — Modern Japanese Art from the Meiji Restoration to the Present. New York, Hacker.
1965 — Zen and Oriental Art. Rutland, Vermont, and Tokyo, Charles E. Tuttle.

Narasaki, Muneshige
1966 — The Japanese Print: Its Evolution and Essence. Tokyo, Kodansha.

Sansom, George
1963 — A History of Japan 1615–1867. Stanford, California, Stanford University Press.

Scheurleer, D. F. Lunsingh
1974 — Chinese Export Porcelain: Chine de Commande. New York, Pitman.

Schmidt, Eberhard
1966 — "Geschichte der Strafrechtspflege", in *Handwörterbuch der Kriminologie*, I, 317 f. Berlin, De Gruyter.

Sheldon, Charles D.
1973 — "Feudal Japan: Politics and Society from the Eighteenth Century to 1868", in Toynbee (1973), 195–224.

Takahashi, Seiichiro
1972 — Traditional Woodblock Prints from Japan. New York and Tokyo, Weatherhill and Heibonsha.

Thompson, Reuben R. (pseud. Ballon Monté)
1975 — The Siege of Paris September 1870 – January 1871. n. l., n. d.

Tjong, Zong Uk
1972 — "Zur Geschichte der Kodifikation des Strafrechts in Ostasien", in *Zeitschrift für die gesamte Strafrechtswissenschaft*, 84 (4): 1088–1119.

Tokoro, Kazuhiro
1969 — A Comparative Analysis of Delinquency Control in Japan and the United States. Unpublished paper.

Tokyo, City of, ed.
1963 — Tokyo-shi Shiko (A Sketchy History of the City of Tokyo). Tokyo.

Toriumi, T.
1973 — "A New Role for Japan: The Meiji Revolution and Its Sequel", in Toynbee (1973), 293–318.

Toynbee, Arnold,
1973 — Half the World: The History and Culture of China and Japan. London, Thames and Hudson.

United Nations
1977 — World Crime Trends. New York, United Nations.

1959 — see Hess 1959

Yinger, M. J.
1960 "Contraculture and Subculture", in *American Sociological Review*, 25: 625f.

Yoshino, Sakuzo
1929 Meiji Bunka Zenshu (All the Writings on Meiji Culture). Tokyo.

INDEX

Figures in roman type refer the reader to the page of the text on which the subject appears; figures *in italics* refer to the plates and to the accompanying captions.

ACKNOWLEDGEMENTS

This book owes a great debt for valuable contributions made by a large number of friends on three continents. Too numerous to be mentioned here each and all, these friends may be assured of our sincere thankfulness. For reading our manuscript and for providing us with frank criticism and most useful suggestions, we wish to express our gratitude in particular to the following (in alphabetical order): Rafael Beermann, University of Freiburg i. B.; Dr. Thomas Enderle, Max-Planck-Institute for Foreign and International Penal Law; Dr. A. Ishii, Tokyo; Dr. K. Ishii, Tokyo; Professors H. H. Jescheck and G. Kaiser, Co-Directors of the Max-Planck-Institute for Foreign and International Penal Law; Ping Lee, Esq., New York; Professor J. Llompart, Sophia University; Professor H. Nakamura, Tokyo; Professor K. Nakayama, Kyoto University; Professor Dr. Nelly Naumann, Director, Institute of Japanese Studies, University of Freiburg; Professor H. Shimizu, Keo University; Professor Z. U. Tjong, Max-Planck-Institute of Foreign and International Penal Law, and Professor K. Tokoro, Rikkyo University.

Furthermore, Robin Rubin edited the text, Julia Kao Hess compiled the index, and Kathleen Nichols typed the manuscript. The photographic work was done by the Audio-Visual Department of the State University of New York College at Brockport (Dr. Gordon Bemis, Director; P. Schlau and M. Wittenstein, Photographers).

Last but by no means least, our gratitude goes to the institutions who helped us so much through their libraries and in many other ways: the State University of New York College at Brockport, the University of Central Florida and the Japan Society.

July 1977 Albert G. Hess Shigeyo Murayama

PLATES

The following plates are considerably enlarged from the original to the size in which they are shown. Unavoidably certain small imperfections were also enlarged. In order to preserve historical faithfulness, no retouching has been attempted.

詿違罪目

七十箇條

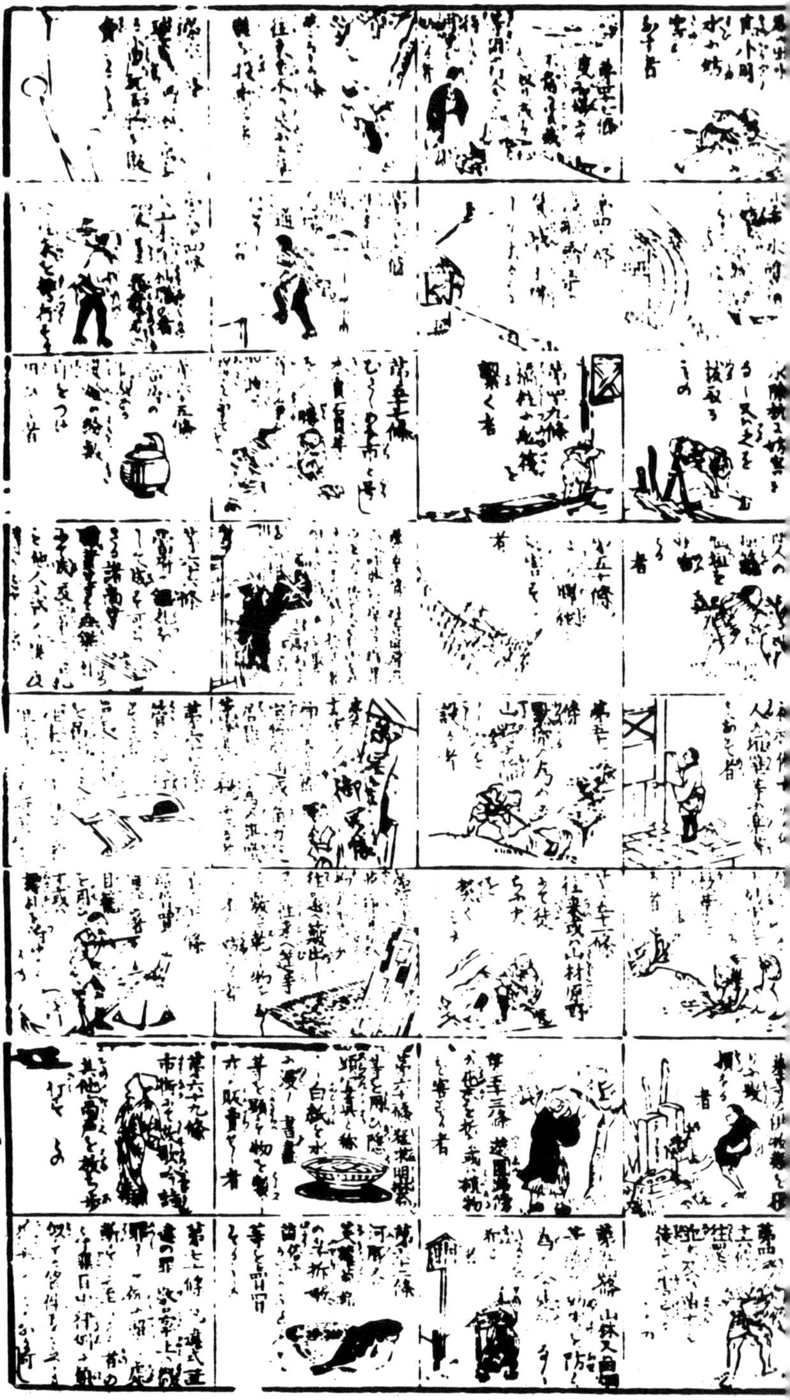

繋ぐ者
第六十九條
其他商品を
第七十條

Kaii Zaimoku Nanajū Kajō. Total view of woodcut by an unknown artist, 1878.

第一條
狭隘の小路と
馬車にて馳
走する者

1

Forbidden is to drive vehicles at high speed in narrow and small streets.

A man on horse-back in European attire and a man-powered cart meet in a narrow street. The rider appears to make a critical remark at the speeding cart puller who stares back at him.

第二〻條 夜中無燈にて諸車を挽き又ハ乗馬する者
但陸軍の諸兵非常の警戒ある時ハ勿論軍隊を組夜陰行進及ひ定制ある徽章の服帽を着用ハ騎とも此限ニ非す

2

Forbidden is during an emergency to pull vehicles or to ride horses at night, [even] with a lighted lantern. Excepted are soldiers in possession of emergency orders who, it is understood, march in the usual formation and wear uniforms and headgear as prescribed for night marches.

Under a night sky, formed by calligraphy, with the half moon in the upper left corner, a ricksha with a lady passenger is traveling during the forbidden hours. Because this ordinance was issued only a short time after the so called Seinan War in 1877, the last uprising of the *samurai* against the government troops, it is not surprising to find a number of security measures for preventing future uprisings. Here civilians are forbidden to drive or ride at all during night-time emergencies.

第三條
斟酌なく
馬車を疾驅
せしめて
行人へ
迷惑を
掛けし
こもの

3

Forbidden is to wantonly drive a coach in such a way as to annoy pedestrians.

A Western-style coach causes a pedestrian laden with goods to tumble by the street side. Passenger and coachman look with concern at the accident.

第四條
馬車及ひ人力車荷車等を往来ニ置き行人の妨をなし及ひ牛馬を街衢ニ横へ行人を妨けし者

4

Forbidden is to impede passersby by leaving rickshas, carts or other vehicles [unattended], or by letting horses or cattle loose in the street.

A cart and a saddled horse are left unattended in the street. Beneath the saddle the horse wears a piece of cloth bearing the family crest of the owner, see also plates 25, 26 and 28.

第五條
荷車及ひ人力車行逢ふ節行くよ迷惑を掛けし者

5

Forbidden is to annoy pedestrians by passing carts.

While two carts are passing by, a person (child?) is thrown on the ground. A lady in a *kimono* with a big sash (*obi*) on her back hurries to help the fallen victim.

第六條
荷車及ひ人力車等を並べ挽き通行と妨けし

6

Forbidden is to block the traffic by carts, rickshas and other vehicles moving side-by-side.

Two carts with large (iron?) wheels, heavily loaded with goods, are being pulled alongside each other.

第七條
行人に強て車馬駕籠等を勧め過言を申掛の

7

Forbidden is to coerce an individual to hire a richsha, horse, or sedan chair or to ask an unusually high fare.

An unwilling lady with a Japanese umbrella (*kasa*) is urged by a ricksha-man with more than desirable insistence to take a ride in his vehicle.
The term "ricksha" is a contraction of the Japanese word *jinrikisha* meaning "man-powered vehicle". It was invented in 1869 in Tokyo and could carry one or two passengers (Koyama, 1961, 1128).

第八條
諸車無番號の
代遵守し其人
其車ニ提燈
無事故屬名
番號を記せざることの
但途中破れ或ハ途中ニ
於て不得止事ある
その限りにあらず

め八

8

Forbidden is to drive a vehicle without a number and without a lantern indicating the owner's address, except when the lantern is broken, or when using another person's lantern in an emergency.

The picture shows a ricksha and a paper lantern, the script indicates the family name Yamaki.

第九條
斃獸ノ死スル者
或ハ汚穢の物
又ハ塵芥を
往来等へ投棄
する者

9

Forbidden is to litter streets with dead animals, filth, and garbage.

Under a European style street lamp a dead dog, fish bones, and other garbage are strewn about.

第十條 戯ニ依り人ニ汚穢物及ひ石礫等を抛澆らしことの

10

Forbidden is to throw, due to rudeness, excrements, stones, or similar things at a person, even if that person has shown objectionable behavior.

A man throws a stone at a child who may have done some mischief and is running away.

第十一條
婦人(ふじん)にて謂れなく断髪(ざんぱつ)するもの

11

Forbidden is for women to cut their hair without grounds.

Paradoxically our ordinance coincides with the publication of the Japanese translation of John Stuart Mill's *On the Subjection of Women.*

第十二條

市中糞尿運搬無鑑札ニて糞水用ひす運搬する者ゝ日の出一時前限うると犯するもの

12

Forbidden is to transport urine or excrement without disinfectant less than one hour before sunrise except with a license to do so.

While the sun is rising in the upper left a man is about to remove containers of excrement from a house.

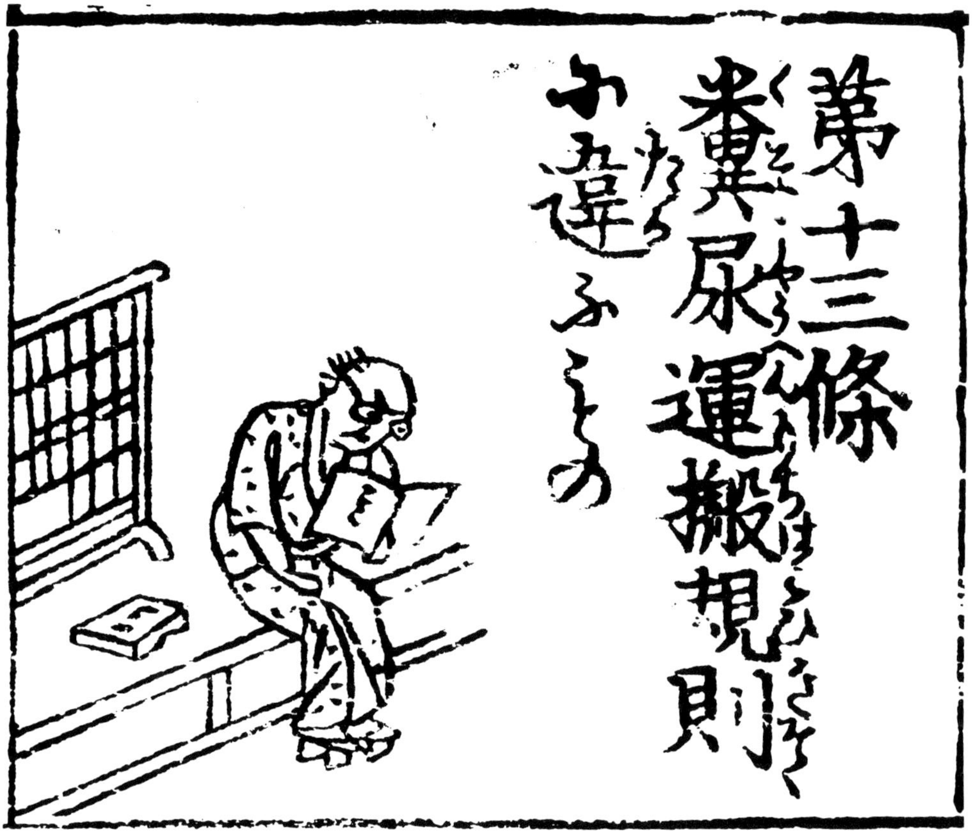
第十三條
糞尿運搬規則
に違ふことの

13

Forbidden is to violate the rules regarding the removal of excrements or urine.

A man is reading the regulations on sanitation. Wearing *yukata* (a light type of kimono) and European-style eyeglasses, he sits in front of a screen on the elevated part of the room which is covered by straw-mats (*tatami*). On the *tatami* one does not wear shoes. His feet, in wooden clogs (*geta*) rest on the floor of the entrance-way (*doma*) on which straw-mats are not laid.
When the regulations were promulgated Japan had just suffered an epidemic of cholera, therefore sanitary provisions were of importance.

第十四條

市中往来筋に於て便所に非さる場所に大小便をする者

14

Forbidden is to urinate or defecate in such places on city streets that are not [public] toilets.

A kimono-clad man, who appears to be singing merrily, urinates in front of a house.

第十五條
宿屋渡世の者
止宿人名を記
載せて或ハ之を
届出て可との

15

Forbidden is for an innkeeper not to record and report the name of a guest.

In the guest room of a Japanese-style hotel (*ryokan*) a guest is sitting on a cushion with an old-fashioned ashtray in front of him. Across from him kneels the inn-keeper who is subserviently asking the guest's name in order to write it into the guest-register that is before him. Next to the register are a lantern and a brush-and-ink stand. In the background at the left is the *tokonoma*, that part of a Japanese room which is devoted to embellishment. A *kakemono* (scroll) is hanging on the wall. Below it lies the traveler's round flat hat.

第十六條
旅籠屋
渡世ならずして人を
止宿せしめ
届け
出さる者

16

Forbidden is for a person whose regular occupation is not that of keeping an inn to lodge a person and not to report him.

A traveler holding his round flat hat, is asking a kneeling person (obviously not an inn-keeper) for lodging, and the latter appears to reply "*dozo*" (please). At the right is a *hibachi*, a charcoal heater. Travelers are always depicted in these pictures with their characteristic traveler's hat and with dark stripes on the legs, indicating leggings.

第十七條
宿引と
唱へ無
實の言
を以て旅
人に迷惑を
掛し〳〵の

17

Forbidden is to mislead travelers about an inn through untruthful advertising.

A rich traveler is accompanied by his servant who is carrying boxes in front and back dangling from a pole. The traveler is approached by a "tout" in the business.

第十八條
役人は
合力
等を
申掛る
ことめ

18

Forbidden is to solicit pedestrians for gifts of money or other things.

A beggar is asking for a gift. The reluctant donor on the right is wearing a kimono and carrying a Western-style umbrella.

第九條　往来筋の
番号又ハ人家の番号
名札看板等を戯ニ
破毀するもの

19

Forbidden is to damage, for amusement, street numbers, house numbers, sign posts, and similar objects.

A man removes the name plate of the owner from a house. Until the present day name plates were considered to bring luck and students collected them before examinations.

第二十條

往来常燈を戯に消滅する者

20

Forbidden is to extinguish street lights for amusement.

A tall man blows out a European-style gas lantern.

第廿一條
喧嘩口論に及ひ人の道路を妨け且驚愕させ可き騒動を爲し出せる者

21

Forbidden is to annoy persons and obstruct their freedom of movement by surprising them with insults or attacks.

The picture is not quite clear. Apparently the man in the rear is attacking the man in front. He is holding in his right hand an elongated object (stick? knife?). The surprised victim is attempting to defend himself by grabbing the end of the attacker's left arm and the object. Both men wear kimonos which are rolled up to the hips as customary with the Japanese working class.

第廿二條
猥に他人の争論に荷擔すること

22

Forbidden is to participate in a brawl among strangers without reason.

The man on the left who has a towel over his head is joining the fight in Japanese fashion: he is removing his kimono, probably to show off an elaborate tatoo as a symbol of strength. The persons on the right have already rolled up their sleeves.

第十三條
田園穡藝の
路あらさる
場を
通行し
又ハ牛馬を牽入
る者

23

Forbidden is to walk in cultivated fields outside of footpaths or to lead horses and cattle into such fields.

A peasant carrying a bag is trespassing in a field.

第廿四條
牧場(まきば)外(ほか)を
猥(みだ)りに
牛馬(ぎうば)を
放(はな)チ飼(かひ)
にする者

24

Forbidden is to let horses and cattle wander and graze outside of the pasture without reason.

Two unbridled horses have been allowed to roam around freely. One of them is grazing.

第廿五條
誤て牛馬を放ち他人の田圃及ひ物品を損害する
その

25

Forbidden is to negligently damage another person's real estate or movable property by letting horses and cattle loose.

A runaway horse is damaging fields. The long reins trailing indicate that it got out of the owner's control. Here and in plate 4, 26 and 28, the cloth around the horse's belly carries the crest of the owner.

第廿六條
態て牛馬を放入
家業を食しめ者

26

Forbidden is to let horses and cattle enter into houses by negligently letting them loose.

A horse running loose enters a house, with its reins trailing.

第廿一條
牛馬牽綱三尺に
限るを背
くの

27

Forbidden is to lead cattle by ropes more than three *shaku* long.

A peasant is depicted with a cow trailing a long rope. A *shaku* is 30.3 centimeters or 12.12 inches long. Thus the permissible maximum length of the rope is 90.9 centimeters or 3 feet 4 inches.

第廿八條
狂悪の
牛馬を
知て
飼置く
者

28

Forbidden is to keep wild horses or cattle with foreknowledge of their [wild] nature.

The owner tries to control an excited pack-horse.

第廿九條
總て電信柱に牛馬を繫ぎ或ハ破毀する者

29

Forbidden is to tie up a horse or cattle to a marker, or to damage a stone-marker.

A saddled horse is tied to a marker, used in Japan as a signpost and for other geographic markings.

第三十條
犬を闘ハしめ及ひ
戯に人に
嗾る者

30

Forbidden is to let dogs fight, or to let them bark at persons for amusement.

A peasant tries to stop two fighting dogs with a big stick.

第卅一條
他人の獣
畜類等か
犬を嗾し
掛る者

31

Forbidden is to encourage dogs to chase another persons' animals.

A young person is urging a dog to chase chickens.

第廿二條 飼犬ハ飼主の姓名札を附けさる者又ハ狂犬ニ罹る犬を其侭飼置く他の人畜ニ妨害をなす者

32

Forbidden is to fail to provide a dog with a tag that indicates its owner's name, or to keep a dog without treatment that is sick with rabies so that it harms men and animals.

A dog wears a big name tag around its neck.

第卅三條
巨大の紙鳶を揚け妨害をなすもの

33

Forbidden is to cause disturbance by flying large kites.

A young man is carrying a big kite on his back with the ropes trailing behind. Flying kites is a popular amusement for Japanese children, particularly around New Year's.

第卅四條
車馬
往来の妨碍を

34

Forbidden is to interfere with horse and vehicle traffic while one is under the influence of alcohol or for amusement.

A man, presumably drunk, is annoying the driver of a cart. The drunken person appears to be carrying a bundle of branches on his back. He may be returning from celebrating, with plenty of sake, the Spring or Fall season.

第十七條
雜魚乾
場ヲ妨害
となす
者

35

Forbidden is to disturb a place where fishes are laid out for drying.

With his umbrella a passer-by pulls away fishes that are spread out on a mat for drying.

第卅六條
他人の獵場ヲ妨害する者

36

Forbidden is to interfere with another person's hunting grounds.

A man releases a hare from a trap. He is dressed as a traveler and carries a *furoshiki*, a package wrapped in a kerchief on his shoulder.

第九十七條

他人(たにん)の魚簗(やな)を

等ち妨害(ばうがい)せる

えとみ

37

Forbidden is to interfere with another person's fish traps or with similar objects.

A man disturbs fish traps by means of a long stick.

第廿八條
田畝中ニ
瓦礫
竹木
等と
投入る者

38

Forbidden is to throw pieces of stones, broken glasses, bricks, bamboo-sticks, and other things into rice fields or on the footpaths between the fields.

Japanese peasants, like their counterparts in other countries, have occasional feuds with their neighbors. The man depicted is dumping small objects on the property of his foe.

第卅九條

養田水其外用水ヲ妨害をなす者

39

Forbidden is to interfere with the irrigation of rice fields, or with other watering devices.

Here a farmer is shown in the act of "stealing" water by re-directing its flow from its original destination to his own field. The cultivation of rice is a principle feature of Japanese agriculture and proper irrigation of rice fields is of extreme importance. Even nowadays villagers arrange for continuous watch over their water supply in a cooperative fashion so that nobody can unlawfully take water from another farmer's field.

第四十條
水碓外用水
妨害

40

Forbidden is to interfere with a water-wheel, its grinding apparatus, or the water conduct.

A man is throwing a rock into a water mill.

第十一條
水除杭は妨害を
なし又ハ之を
抜取る
ことの

41

Forbidden is to tamper with poles that stem water [pressure], or to pull them out.

This peasant apparently does not like the water pressure as it is, so he is trying to dislodge the poles. The mechanism of this primitive "dam" works in such a fashion that when the poles are removed, the water pressure decreases and the water flows freely.

第四十一條 他人の植籬圍垣を損毀する者

42

Forbidden is to damage another person's hedges.

A man is pulling out plants or branches from a hedge.

第四十三條

神祠佛堂亦ハ他人の垣壁等ニ楽書たくあそて者

43

Forbidden is to scribble on shrines, temples or on another person's walls.

A person dressed as a traveler holds an old-fashioned inkpot in his left hand and smears graffiti by means of a brush held in his right hand.

第四十四條

他人の行木に妨害をなし又ハ枝葉を拾ひ取る者

Forbidden is to damage another person's bamboo plants or trees or to pick up fallen branches and leaves.

A man, with a *tenugue* (Japanese towel). tied under his chin in peasant fashion, is collecting branches or leaves. Fallen branches and leaves were valuable in old Japan as fuel.

第四十五條 他人の墳墓寺の供物類を猥りに毀損する者

45

Forbidden is to damage any gravesite offerings or to express verbal abuse at another person's tomb or in similar places.

In a cemetery, a man kicks off grave-side offerings, (such as food and flowers) with his right foot. Behind the tombstones stand long boards usually used for inscribing religious texts.

第四十六條
往還の並木及ひ苗木を徒らに害すること

46

Forbidden is to damage young trees or trees in the streets without reason.

A man in a rolled-up kimono is cutting down young trees.

第四十七條
渡船場にて
不當の賃銭
を取り或は
等閑に行人を
待しめ
通便を
妨ぐる者

47

Forbidden is to charge an unduly high price for a ferry ride, or to hinder the transportation of waiting-passengers by neglect.

Two would-be ferry boat passengers – one in a *kimono* carrying a Western-style umbrella, and the other sitting with two packages of goods beside him – are waiting for the over-due ferry boat and berating the boatman who keeps them waiting. The ferry boat can be seen on the other side of the river in the upper righthand corner. tied up in front of the boatman's house. Note the placement of calligraphy so as to represent the body of water.

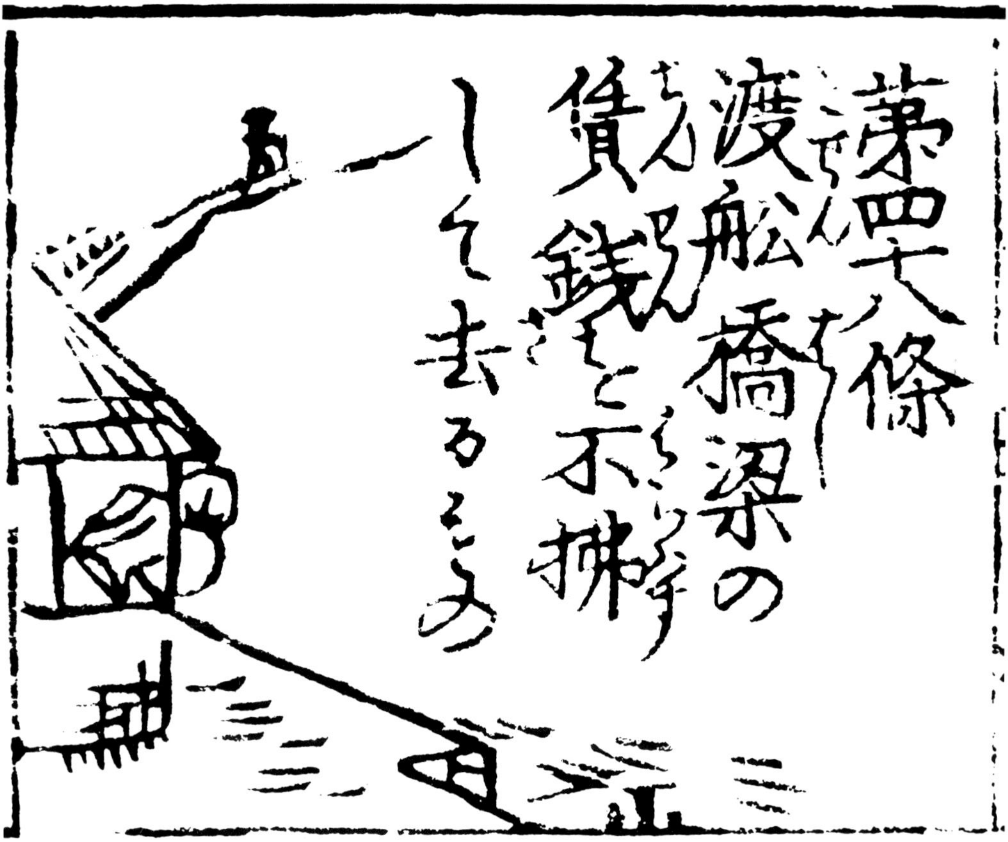

第四七條
渡船橋梁の賃錢を不拂して去ること

48

Forbidden is to walk away without paying the fare for a ferry ride or toll for crossing a bridge.

The man in the left foreground gazes helplessly at the far-away person who has walked away without paying his fare or toll.

第卌九條
橋柱に船筏を繫く者

49

Forbidden is to tie boats and rafts on bridge pillars.

A boatman is tying his boat to the pillar of a wooden bridge.

第五十條
他ノ曝網ヲ妨害スル者

50

Forbidden is to interfere with another person's net while it is laid out for drying.

A man is manipulating a fishing net hung up to dry.

第五十一條

獸攫の為め山野に陥し穴を設る者

51

Forbidden is to dig pits on mountain sides for trapping animals.

A man is digging a pit by means of a hoe.

第五十一條
往来或ハ山林原野於て徒ちに火を焚くこと

52

Forbidden is to make fires for amusement in streets, forests or fields.

A man dressed as a traveler, with his hat and cane in front of him, enjoys himself by the side of a bonfire.

第五十三條 遊園路傍
ノ花木を折り或ハ植物
など害する者

53

Forbidden is to break off branches or to damage plants in public parks or along streets.

A man in a *kimono* and a Western-style hat is breaking a big branch off a tree. See comments on this custom on page 39 of the text.

第五十四條　山林又ハ田畑等ニ於て妨害を防ぐ為に人の建設すしるを犯を者

54

Forbidden is to violate the prohibitions expressed on signs erected for the protection of forests, cultivated fields, etc.

A man is pulling down the rope fencing off private grounds. At the left one can see the sign presumably forbidding his act.

第五十五條

往来並木の枝に古草鞋を投掛る者

55

Forbidden is to throw old rice-straw sandals on the branches of trees along the streets.

A man is shown in the act of throwing an old sandal up on a tree. The reasons for this prohibition are obscure. It has been suggested that its purpose was to suppress superstition. The throwing of an object on to a tree is sometimes undertaken as a means of divination.

第五十六條
往来止の
掲示ある場を通行せし
者

56

Forbidden is to pass through a place where there are signs that prohibit it.

A man in his kimono with rolled-up sleeves, wearing a pair of *getas*, walks past a no trespassing sign.

第五十七條

むさしめ多市と号し木實石貝等を以て勝負を争ひ賭博の様とみえて その

57

Forbidden is to play the so-called *musashi-anaichi* by using nuts, stones, shells, etc. competing for victory or defeat which indicates gambling.

Two men are engaged in this popular gambling game.

第五十八條　社寺開扉縁日及ヒ諸興行席等群集の場所ニ於テ人の自由を妨け或ハ木戸銭を払ハさる者
但木戸銭を取る興行主ニ下ケ渡ス

Forbidden is to disturb others while they attend religious festivals, public performances, and similar events, or not to pay admission, except when the admission fee goes into the coffers of the management of the performance.

In front of an extrance to a theatre a ticket-seller sits behind a box marked "Admission". At the left is a customer wearing a Japanese *haori*, or a coat, but sporting a Western hat to show he is a man of fashion. On both sides over the entrance are Japanese characters only partly visible, apparently advertising names of performers.

第五十九條

神仏開扉の節宝物弘通或ハ角力芝居興行人の為め旗幟を寺詣場外ニ掲ケ立ル者

59

Forbidden is to raise banners, flags, etc. advertising religious festivals with exhibitions of treasures, or performances of wrestlers or actors at places other than where these events are to take place.

Two banners, both displaying the inscription "Religious Festival" are shown. A lady strolls by and an old man walks with a cane in hand.

萬十條
菜種并穀
物其他方先
往還へ筵出し
又ハ往来へ筵手
を敷き乾し物をあ
往来を妨る者

60

Forbidden is to spread out medicine seeds, grains and so forth in front of stores or to disturb the traffic by drying things on strawmats in streets.

Medicinal herbs or plants are being dried on a straw mat on the ground while textile fabrics are stretched on boards standing at right in an inclined position. In old Japan this stretching of fabrics substituted for the modern ironing.

第六十一條 猛嘗明君

茸を用ひ隠顕写眞と称白紙を水に渡し書畫

茸を顕もて物を製し亦ハ販賣せし者

61

Forbidden is to conceal words and pictures or make them invisible on white paper by the process called "photography", i. e. by means of mercury, chromium potassium sulfate, other chemicals, and water baths and to sell such photographs.

It may appear somewhat strange to-day to learn that Japan – nowadays, the World's largest supplier of photographic goods – once forbade photography. One can only speculate on the reasons for doing so. As pointed out above (see p. 20), photo studios were then operated by the Japanese government. Therefore one may think that this prohibition was enacted to protect the state monopoly. If so, however, legislation would more likely have been nation-wide, not left to the provinces. A likelier explanation would be military. As has been pointed out repeatedly, Japan was then recovering from the various ex-samurai rebellions, and especially from the Seinan War (see plate 2). The Japanese had also closely observed the Franco-Prussian War of 1870/71 (see above p. 30). It was this latter war during which photography played – probably for the first time – a military role. The role was dramatic and widely publicized: Besieged and surrounded, Paris received communications from the rest of France by means of microphotographed messages that were transported by carrier pigeons (Thompson, 1975, 258 f.). It would have been quite understandable if the Japanese authorities wanted to prevent any such use of photography should future emergencies occur.

第六十二條
河豚又ハ
菜蘿葍類
の芽折嫩
苗俗ニうひこりちうとくさし
等を賣買
するこゝと〻の

62

Forbidden is to sell or buy globefish or [poisonous] vegetable sprouts and similar products.

The dried blown-up skin of the globefish is sometimes sold in curio shops as lampshades. The globefish can be a delicacy, if prepared properly. Otherwise its consumption can be deadly because it is poisonous.

第六十三條

球首或ハ西洋紙と唱ふる小兒玩弄物を販賣るもの

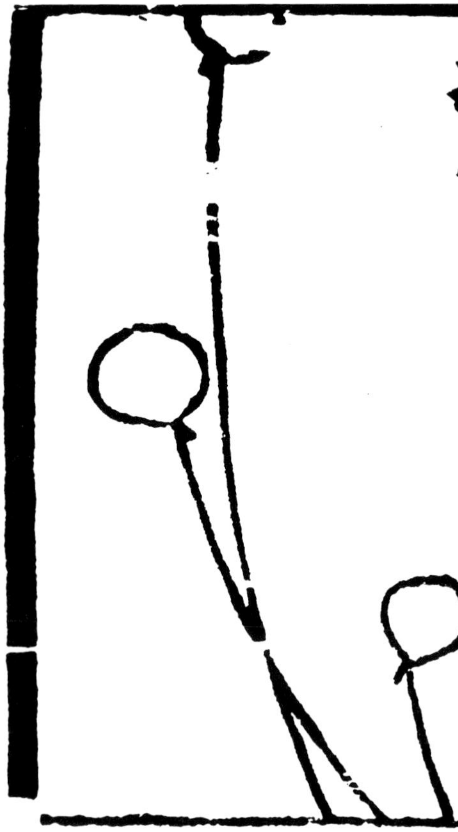

63

Forbidden is to sell balloons or children's toys made of so-called "Western Paper".

Military reasons similar to those discussed in plate 61, may have been responsible for the interdiction against toy balloons. Balloons, though mostly large, manned balloons, had also been used during the Franco-Prussian War (1870/71). They transported the first airmail pigeons and messengers out of besieged Paris and were used for observing the enemy. Occasionally even toy balloons were put to service (Thompson, 1975, *passim*; s. p. 77 on toy balloons).

第六十四條

大工木挽杣職の者鋸斧等の類露刃の儘往來を携行する者

64

Forbidden is for carpenters, woodcutters and timbermen, to carry saws or axes without covers in the streets.

A carpenter, or someone of a similar vocation, carries an ax.

第六十五條
當府の
制規ある
提燈に紛敷
印をつけ
用ひし者

65

Forbidden is to install or use lanterns with a design that can be mistaken for symbols of the Government.

The woodcut shows a lantern generally used to display the name of ownership.

第二十六條

當府の鑑札なくして成を可らざる諸商業職業等を無鑑札ニて成し及び名前の許鑑札を他人ニ貸又ハ譲渡等をなせし者

Forbidden is to undertake a business without a license from the competent authority, or to practise without such licenses occupations that require them, or to lend or sell licenses.

The picture is that of a document, obviously a license.

第六十七條

管外へ旅行する者戸長へ往帰と届出て又ハ往来券を申請する者

但日帰の者此限に非ず

67

Forbidden is to fail to report to the town mayor travel beyond the town limits, or to fail to apply for a passport except in the case of a one-day trip.

The ubiquitous traveler's hat with its ribbons for tying around the chin, and a document, representing a passport, are depicted.

第六十八條
紙屑買渡世の者目籠に形を用ひす或ハ籠に標札を附けさるもの

68

Forbidden is for the junktrade to operate without a scale or a license tag.

A junk-dealer holds a scale by his teeth. He is weighing a piece of his wares. On the ground, on both sides of the dealer, are packages filled with junk. Holding the scale by the teeth, the dealer customarily wants to appear "honest". It is done to show that he is not manipulating the scale by his fingers.

第六十九條

市街にて放歌吟詩其他高声を放ち歩行候もの

69

Forbidden is to sing songs, recite poems, or make unpleasant noises while walking in a city.

By moonlight, a man with his mouth open is making undesirable noises. The towel on his head may indicate that he has just emerged from a public bath in a relaxed mood.

第七十條　違式註違の罪ハ警察上の職權として例ニ照し處斷する二至る者の其罪目中律例ニ類似する條件あるとも抵觸ある可し

All cases of *ishiki* and *kaii* will be decided by the police without going to court and without reference to precedents. In case similar provisions are found in earlier law, they shall not be applied under any circumstances.

The last item does not add another petty offense but stipulates the exclusive jurisdiction of the police for *ishiki* and *kaii*. Petty offenses did not come before the judiciary. Furthermore it is stipulated that this ordinance over-rules previous law; the police when acting in a judicial capacity, is not bound by previous decisions.